God's Designing

R.E. Clark

GnG Publishers
122 Skinner St.
Centerton, AR 72719

First Edition
Published by GnG Publishers
9/1/2014

Printed in the United States of America
Cover photo courtesy: StockPhotosforFree.com
ISBN-13: 978-0692281604
ISBN-10: 0692281606

Table of Contents

ACKNOWLEDGMENTS

This book has been written over many years even though it only took a matter of months to put the words down on paper. Through the years in which God was preparing my heart to write, He was allowing me the privilege of being blessed by faithful friends and family who openly and freely shared their insights with me. All of you have helped me write, though you may not have known you were serving in such a role.

You have encouraged me by your steadfast walk with Jesus, your reassurances given in so many ways that they could never be listed in this limited space, and the fact that you are reading this book.

I am grateful to my daughter, Kayre Chastain, who has served once again as my proofreader and honest editor. I appreciate the fact that she is willing to offer helpful criticism to her daddy when his thoughts do not convey properly as the words are written upon paper.

Thanks must be given to my wife, Trudy, who allows me the time to write and create my books literally from the ground up through GnG Publishing.

Of course, I thank each of you who have been faithful readers since my first book, *Glasses In the Grass*, was released.

PREFACE

This is a day of easy believing. Decisions for Jesus are often made with a flippancy that leaves much to be desired. Prayers for salvation are little more than some formula created to make a person feel better about their present condition.

After writing the first book in this series, *God's Leading*, I began to think about what I would write next. At that moment I only was thinking about another book—not a series. It was in this period of time that I concluded that my next book would be about the evidences for the Christian life.

My hope is that this book will serve two purposes. The first is that after reading this book you will be more convinced than ever before that you really are a believer—a follower of Jesus Christ as His disciple. The second reason I have written *God's Designing* is to help some come to the full understanding that they simply have never been born again. You may have had an experience that raised your religious awareness, but when all is weighed against the truth of God's word, you simply are not a Christian.

At the end of each chapter is a set of questions that I call mileposts. These will serve to help you evaluate your present journey through life and will help you to discern whether you are truly a part of God's Designing.

I pray that believers will be strengthened and the lost saved because of this book!

Chapter One

THE PLAN

John "Hannibal" Smith, the leader of the A-Team always said at the end of each episode, "I love it when a plan comes together!"

So do I.

Planning has always been a strong point in my life. I not only love it when a plan comes together—I love to plan! I think that you will more than likely love the outcome when you have spent the time necessary to plan.

Have you ever considered the planning that went into God's design for your life? More than just for your life as it is lived out for a set number of days. But your life for eternity and specifically your life as a Christian.

Before you can even begin to make an attempt at grasping the concept of God as a designer, you must find some place to call the beginning. For us as mere mortals, we need, or at the least I need, a timeline. We simply do not function well in the realms of eternity.

I have good news and bad news for you. I can give you hints about the beginning of things, but since I am locked away in mortality, I am powerless to take you all the way back to the moment it all began. I can, however, take you to the place where it all began.

That place is none other than the mind of God. Yes, that was a shudder that you felt deep inside and the hair just raised a bit on the nape of your neck. Attempting to convey or to understand such a subject as the mind of God will cause most to pause and reconsider. But there is simply no other place to begin.

It was here in the mind of God that the concept of the church and its constituents, the Christians, were conceived. Very simply put, God had a plan and everything that has taken place since that plan began in His mind has been moving that plan toward completion.

We are introduced to the concept of the church through the words of Jesus as recorded in the gospel of Matthew, "And I also say to you that you are Peter, and on this rock I will build My church, and the gates of Hades shall not prevail against it." (Matthew 16:18)

Here, in this moment of recorded history, God reveals His plan. He intends to build a church here on earth. Not a physical building, but instead a community of believers that have been called out of this world's system.

The very word that was used by Jesus and translated as church means "called out." The word in Greek is ecclesia. It speaks of the church universally and not of the local churches that we are so familiar with today.

In this first revelation of God's plan, He establishes the foundation for the church which is Jesus Himself. Then He promises that His plan for the church would never be thwarted. Though we are not told exactly when God's designing of the church and the Christians who would compose its body began, we can make some assumptions from later texts.

In Paul's letter to the Ephesians he writes to the saints gathered there. The term saints is used to designate the Christians who were gathered in each of these localities and were a part of the church as a whole. Paul tells the Ephesians, "just as He chose us in Him before the foundation of the world, that we should be holy and without blame before Him in love," (Ephesians 1:4)

So there you have it. God had already chosen the inhabitants of the church long before He declared that there would even be a church. He did so before there was a world in which it would exist or there were people to be a part of its embodiment. The beginning of the plan was in the mind of the eternal God.

His designing was not contingent on circumstances since it all took place outside of the constraints of time. His plan was perfect because it came from a perfect mind. His purpose would be fulfilled based upon the assurance that there was only one will to consider: His own.

Everything that God designed in the entire universe was planned to accommodate His grand design—the church. His creation of mankind was to populate His church. His call to repentance was to prepare His church. His only begotten Son came as the Christ to redeem His church. One glorious day He will extend the greatest call of all as He raptures His church out of this world and delivers her without spot or blemish into His eternal presence.

So His design will be complete. His plan fulfilled. His will accomplished. But until then, there is much work to be done.

Christians are living in a world that is becoming less accommodating by the day. Though we are still greatly protected here in the West, thousands are dying as martyrs around the globe each day.

Evidences for Christianity are being called for in the public square. Many doubt whether Christians have any right to claim their special relationship with the God who designed their very existence.

We need not fret over these demands that come from a world that can never understand what it means to be a Christian until they themselves become one. However, we do have a set of evidences that can be considered.

An examination of these truths will have two effects. First, they will solidify what you believe as a Christian and a member of the body of called out ones: the church. These evidences will serve as checkpoints in the life of the Christian. Like mileposts along a highway, you can use each of these validations to check on your progress.

Second, as these truths are lived out on a daily basis in front of a doubting world, that same world will come to recognize that the church is still alive and well on planet Earth. She may have been ridiculed, abused, accused, and

Mileposts

What plans are you making to better understand who you are as a Christian?

_____

_____

_____

_____

Where did the idea for the church and Christians originate?

_____

_____

_____

_____

What does the word church mean? Where does the church exist?

_____

_____

_____

_____

Where and why were the believers called Christians?

_____

_____

_____

_____

NOTES

Chapter Two

THE PROOF

Prove it!

In a world of get-rich-quick schemes and shady deals it is not unusual for people to demand proof. Although there seems to be a ready source of those who do not demand evidence or validity since the infomercials continue to abound with the recommendation that you call in the next five minutes or the deal goes away forever…right!

In the case of Christianity or the church, (I will use these two terms interchangeably throughout this book) I think it is very appropriate for the world to look at us and say, "Prove it!"

Variety may be the spice of life, but with a different church on every block, the television filled with folks declaring that they have a corner on the Christian brand, and the Internet bursting with websites that lure the unsuspecting into traps of false beliefs, it is time that Christians take an opportunity to offer proof of their claims that they have a relationship with Christ. It simply takes more than a word of testimony to offset the bombardment of false ideas.

Our proof cannot come from an internal source only. To engage in a loop of circular reasoning proves nothing. Declaring that you believe within yourself alone carries little weight in a world of perpetual doubters.

It is time for the ultimate proof of our Christianity and our proclamation that we belong to the church of God. What is needed is a taste of the pudding.

You do know what I mean, don't you?

I grew up with a familiar saying: *The Proof Is In the Pudding.*

This idiom can be traced as far back as the beginning of the 17th century. The shortened form which I grew up quoting actually makes no sense. If the proof is simply in the pudding, there can never be any assurance that it is really proven or that the pudding has any quality to be realized.

The longer phrase is: *The Proof of the Pudding Is In the Eating.*

Now we are getting somewhere. I can declare that the pudding is delicious, one of a kind, etc., but until it is eaten the proof remains unproven and therefore is of no value.

This is exactly where many who declare their connection to Christ fall short of real validated proof in their claim to Christianity and/or relationship with the church. Their proof is in the pudding, but no one is allowed to taste and see if the pudding is good or not.

The world is not only asking; they have every right to do so. Especially when so many are not giving a solid answer to the big **IF.**

Before we assume too much about the word "if", let's get a good working definition for this little, giant word.

Most of you would take the position that "if" is conditional and that it is usually used when doubts prevail. I immediately think of the weather when I consider using the word "if". We will go to the beach **if** it doesn't rain.

We may have listened to the forecast and took stock in the prognostication of the weather man. The evidence of our confidence in his prediction is readily exposed though when we include the little word "if" in our statement.

In the Greek language in which Paul wrote his letter the word "if" does not stand alone as it does in the English translation. The next word "indeed" is included as one word. The translated phrase "if indeed" then is not one of doubt, but one of assumption.

It might be said in a literal sense, "If, by your deeds, you continue, etc." There is an assumption that since our relationship with God has been restored by the work of Christ on the cross there will be a continuing proof of such restoration in our everyday living.

The proof comes in two easily verifiable forms. The first proof of your Christian life will be a continuation. The second is like unto it and is the result of the continuation. That is, you will not be moved and will persevere in a position of hope found in the finished work of Christ.

Continuance is the test of reality. The word carries with it the idea of remaining in a certain state of mind or attitude. Just as we needed a place for the designing work of God to begin, we need a place for it to continue. Paul places our continuance on the firm ground of faith.

The foundation of faith which Paul establishes as the center of our continuation as Christians is a personal faith. Faith speaks of our conviction, confidence, and assurance. It is to be persuaded concerning the facts of salvation and to make a decision to follow Christ. Therefore, it is a declaration to be a Christian.

Here is where it all begins…or should I say continues. God began designing us before the foundation of the world. He continues the fulfillment of His plan on a day by day basis as we continue in the faith.

Hebrews 11:6 makes plain the fact that without faith we cannot please God. The prophet Habakkuk declares, "Behold the proud, his soul is not upright in him; but the just shall live by his faith." (2:4) This verse is directly quoted three times in the New Testament: Romans 1:17, Galatians 3:1, and Hebrews 10:38. If God repeats Himself this many times it must be very, very important.

It simply comes down to belief. You must know what you believe and believe what you know. When this element is settled on the inside of the Christian then it will begin to be evident on the outside of the Christian.

Profession and practice are prevalent in the persevering faith of the Christian. You may find profession without practice, but very little time passes before this profession is proven to have no real basis for believing.

On the other hand, you may find someone who is attempting to practice the Christian life, but has no faith in place. They have no platform upon which to stand. Here too, time will quickly reveal the impossibility of this person being a proven Christian. Only so much can be accomplished in their own strength and when resistance comes they will quickly fade.

I can relate to both of these conditions. Both usually exist in a person who has never become a proven Christian and thereby a part of the body of Christ: the church.

The following is my testimony as I recorded in my first devotional, *Glasses in the Grass*. My early religious years illustrate this idea of being an unproven Christian.

Religion has never been a problem for mankind. In the absence of any formal religious exercise, people have always been able to create a god in their own image and worship that god very well.

This desire to worship is generated by a God-shaped void in the human heart. Nothing will fill that emptiness except a relationship with the God of this universe, but people try everything but God.

I was one of those people. My first experience at making a religious decision came when I was nine years old. My mother had me sit with the pastor who with the best of intentions on both their parts asked me some questions about Jesus and my life.

I had been in church long enough that I had learned the correct answers. I passed the test and the next Sunday was baptized. I had a form of godliness, but lacked the power of a changed life (2 Timothy 3:5.) I was still lost in my sin.

Fast forward sixteen years. I had been faithful most of those years to attend church. I taught the adult men's Sunday School class as a 19 year old. Knowing the content of the Bible was not a problem for me. I loved to study and prepare a lesson. I led the youth department at my church. All of these religious activities were to my credit, but to no avail. I still had that void in my heart that could not be filled.

I began to ask myself and others why I was alive; why was I born here; what was my purpose in life? At this time in my life, I had stopped attending church, but I was still searching.

It was during this search that a dear friend asked if she could take my children to Vacation Bible School. That one act broke my heart! I never thought I would be at the place that someone else would have to bring my children to church.

My children did attend Vacation Bible School that week. My wife and I went to the commencement activities and the next Sunday we were in church as a family. But the emptiness only grew larger.

My questions could not be answered through religious activity. Each sermon seemed aimed directly at me and when an invitation was given to receive Christ as Savior, I would go back to that experience as a nine year old boy.

In my heart, though, I knew that all I had done then was seek to please my mother and my pastor. My emptiness loomed more real than ever, but God was at work in my life.

I owned a grocery business at this time. On a Monday morning in October 1979, I opened my store early as usual and began to prepare for the first customers of the day. All alone in that empty grocery store building, God spoke to my heart. It was not audible, but it may as well have been. "Trust me today. My Son has paid the price for your sin. Come to me."

I knelt behind the deli case of my grocery store and gave my heart and life to Christ that morning. I was gloriously born again.

Everything was new and my questions no longer mattered. There were no bright shining lights. There was no angelic choir singing—only me and God on a grocery store floor.

When I raised my head from praying, I was looking into the back of my deli case. There staring me in the face was a large stick of bologna. I have never forgotten that scene. It was as if God was saying, "R.E., no more bologna for you."

I had lived the life of religious bologna. It did not hold the answer to life's greatest questions. It could not fill the void of my life. Only Jesus could do that...and He did! That's my testimony—what's yours? 'Whoever calls on the name of the Lord shall be saved.' ~ Romans 10:13

Though I had a religious life, I simply did not have the proof needed to confirm that I was a Christian. It became evident to me internally and was surely evident to everyone else externally.

Paul went on to say to the Colossians that this continuance in the faith was secured by being grounded. The idea of being grounded is based on the following principle.

A solid foundation must be designed. Then all of the superstructure of faith is built upon that foundation. From this sure foundation a stability exists that prevents a catastrophic failure and the ultimate exposure of a faulty belief. Jesus gave us a parable that describes the consequences of a poorly designed foundation.

He declared, "Therefore whoever hears these sayings of Mine, and does them, I will liken him to a wise man who built his house on the rock: and the rain descended, the floods came, and the winds blew and beat on that house; and it did not fall, for it was founded on the rock. But everyone who hears these sayings of Mine, and does not do them, will be like a foolish man who built his house on the sand: and the rain descended, the floods came, and the winds blew and beat on that house; and it fell. And great was its fall." (Matthew 7:24-27)

Remember that the foundation of the church and of the Christian is The Rock which is Jesus. The parable of the two builders clearly demonstrates what happens when the house is placed on the wrong foundation. It is not a matter of "if" the house will fall, but when.

Again, we can use the world "if" either way. We can look upon the house built on sand and say, "This house will stand **if** it does not rain." Or we can say, "**If** a house is built upon the rock, it will not fall."

The second statement is the essence of Paul's teaching to the Colossians. They would remain steadfast because they had placed their faith upon the finished foundation of Christ's work on Calvary.

There is another concept of grounding that would not have been understood by the Colossians or Paul for that matter. It deals with grounding as it pertains to electricity.

When dealing with electricity, grounding is very important. Now the subject of this book is not electrical science, but the illustration is valid in this case.

For an electrical current to be used it requires a proper ground. This grounding completes or closes the circuit and the power is released in a controlled process that produces such modern conveniences as lighting.

When there is no proper grounding two things can happen. First, the power may be reduced due to an improper grounding. Second, the current that is traveling along any given wire that is not grounded properly has the capacity to deliver a shock that could prove fatal.

You have probably felt just such a discharge of static electricity when touching a metal object. The discharge is the stored current in your body finding a proper grounding.

Had Paul written these verses in the 21st century he may have said something along these lines: "If you stay grounded in the faith you will not be shocked by the world's current that is flowing all around you."

Earlier I spoke of not being moved from the foundation of hope that comes from a life of faith. This immovability is what gives structure to the Christian life. Two words are used to describe this superstructure that rises upon the foundation of faith.

Paul tells the Colossians they should be steadfast and immovable. It would appear that he is just using synonyms to brace his point in using the phrase, "if indeed." But there is more here than just a repeating of oneself.

The word steadfast describes firm resolve and steadiness. Here you can see a picture of firmness that defies all challenges to a belief based upon faith in the finished work of Christ.

Immovable, on the other hand, speaks of resisting the forces that are attempting to uproot and carry the superstructure of faith somewhere else. Hidden away inside the original word in Greek is the root word from which we get our English word kinetic.

Here we are again with the idea of energy. Instead of static or stored energy, this is an active moving force that is rising against the faith that keeps the Christian secure in his belief.

Just as Jesus described in the parable of the two builders, the rains that come and the flood that rises against the house built upon sand will move it away from its faulty foundation. It is not the foundation that is damaged for the sand will simply resettle after the flooding. The real destruction is to the superstructure built thereon.

All that was seen is carried away and relocated downstream. This relocation by force never leaves that which is moved in its original form. One needs only see the results of modern floods to see the devastation that occurs when the kinetic power of rising waters is brought against a structure built on sinking sand.

This then serves as the proof of our claim to Christianity. If we are not moved away from the hope of the gospel then we prove our salvation to be true. Hope is the ultimate completion of our salvation.

The flood that rises against the Christian today often carries with it the debris of doubt. This doubt arises when we see floating our way some "new gospel." This false gospel will proclaim an easier path to Christianity. It will declare that faith can be built upon mere human effort to reform.

Reformation will never replace regeneration. Our old tilting and tottering structures must be torn down—not only torn down, but the old foundations dug down until they are placed firmly upon The Rock, Jesus Christ.

Paul identified himself as a minister of the gospel. He did not come with some newfangled idea to catch the attention of those who could not care less.

He came proclaiming the same old story that had brought him to his knees on the Damascus Road. Paul's proof was in his changed life.

No longer a Christian hater, but now a Christ herald. No longer a Christian murderer, but now a Christian missionary. Paul's life was so radically changed and the proof so dramatic that even the believers doubted that someone could be changed so radically. But he would not be moved. He steadfastly held to the faith that had rescued him from the shifting sands of religion and placed his feet firmly upon The Rock.

Where is the proof of your Christianity? If you were convicted of the "crime" of Christianity, would there be enough proof to convict you?

Are the storms rocking your world? Are you reeling from every little puff of wind?

Join the chorus of Christians who sing aloud their faith, "On Christ the solid Rock I stand, all other ground is sinking sand. All other ground is sinking sand!"

Mileposts

Why is the world demanding more proof from Christians today?

_____
_____
_____
_____

Being a Christian is best proven from the external. What resource does the Christian have for such proof? Why?

_____
_____
_____
_____

What two possibilities does the author give for defining the word "if"?

_____
_____
_____
_____

What verse is quoted 3 times in the New Testament about faith and where is it found in the Old Testament?

_____
_____
_____
_____

What does the parable of the two builders teach us about the importance of a sure foundation?

_____

_____

_____

_____

What analogy does the author make about the importance of proper grounding?

_____

_____

_____

_____

What were some of the proofs of the Apostle Paul's claim to Christianity?

_____

_____

_____

_____

NOTES

Chapter Three

THE PURPOSE

Once you have rock solid proof of your salvation settled it makes sense to ask the next question: What exactly is the purpose of God saving us and calling us to be Christians?

Purpose may be one of the most misunderstood concepts to consider when thinking about God. As His design for the church and for the Christian is examined, it becomes clear that only a sovereign, eternal God could have brought into existence such organisms with purpose.

The idea of purpose comes from the heart and mind of a creator. Purpose does not particularly belong to God alone. Any person may create, but no person may create without the element of purpose being in place at the outset. This separates the purpose of God from the purposes of men.

God, however, is **the** Creator. He is never at a loss when it comes to creating, because everything created is always done so according to His purpose.

Paul made it very clear concerning the purpose of God as he with bold assurance wrote, "And we know that all things work together for good to those who love God, to those who are the called according to His purpose." (Romans 8:28)

You can clearly see the answer to the dilemma that so many face when things don't seem to be going their way. They simply cannot see how tragedy, heartbreak, or failure can be good. As life unfolds with all of its dark days and ways it is always good, because God's purpose is always at work.

As noted in the previous chapter on the proof for the Christian life, salvation begins in the mind of God before time begins. It is in the mind of God as the Creator that His purpose begins at the very point that He envisioned the Church and those who would become Christians.

This is great news for us! God is never caught by surprise, because nothing can take place apart from His purpose. God never has to say, "Now what?" or "Oops!" His purpose cannot be thwarted. Nor will His purpose be changed.

It may appear to us as individuals that God has multi-purposes at work in the world, but this is not true. There is only one purpose. This is how God sews all of the activity of millions of Christians into one single process, for that process is operating according to His purpose.

Let's imagine for a moment that you sat down with a pencil and sketch pad with the intent to create. You spend days drawing and designing the various parts of your creation.

Then you send your schematic to a shop that has the tools to produce all of the individual parts. A few more days pass and you now have in your possession each piece that can be used to make your creation a reality.

You have a piece of metal tubing that is filled with ink. You have another larger piece of tubing that will hold the ink barrel in place securely. A clip is provided on the instrument which allows you to place it in a pocket and prevent it from falling out when you bend over to pick something up from the floor.

All of the pieces are in place. They are assembled and all meet your specifications as ordered.

At this moment, you place a finger to your temple and ask a ridiculous question, "I wonder what I am going to do with this thing I have created?"

You are probably screaming out to this person, "It's a pen! You've created an ink pen! Can't you see what's right before your face?"

Now you are most likely reasoning correctly that no one in their right mind would invest all of the time and effort to create something without any idea in place of what they had intended to create. This is the principle of purpose.

Purpose always precedes creation. This is especially true with God since He lives in the eternal present as the great I Am. Unlike man when he creates and makes adjustments along the way toward completion, God never has to deviate from His purpose. It is already fulfilled in His mind and all that follows in His creative acts works together for good according to His purpose.

Note that when the recorded acts of creation were given to us in Genesis that after each day's work on God's part, he responded to the creation by evaluating it and saying, "It is good." God's purpose was at work from day one or day one as we know it. His purpose has always been, because He has always been!

And that brings us to the question that opened this chapter: What exactly is the purpose of God in saving us and calling us to be Christians?

You should not assume that I understand completely the mind of God nor that I am attempting to unveil God's entire purpose in designing the church and creating Christians to fulfill His purpose as the body of the church. I do think that there are a few indicators of God's purpose in calling men and women to be Christians that we can readily know.

These identifiers in the Christian life give us assurance that we are indeed a part of God's purpose. All Christians have similar functions because we all are based on the same model.

Think of it this way. When an item is created it is given a model number. That particular model is designed to perform certain functions according to its creative purpose. All individual units that have that model number operate exactly the same.

If you ever need to repair an item, you will need the model number to order the correct parts. This number tells the repairman nearly everything he needs to know about the item. But there is another piece of information that is needed to correctly identify your particular unit. You will need the serial number.

The serial number makes each unit of a certain model unique. If tweaks or upgrades have been added to a model, the serial number will let the repairman know if your item is equipped in a certain way.

Armed with the model number and the serial number, you can make a call to the repair center with the assurance that the person you are speaking with will know exactly what your item looks like. Parts can be ordered to fit and before long you are up and running again.

Here's where I deviate from my analogy. As Christians, we are not just units that have fallen off some conveyor belt. God is not mass producing believers. The church nor the Christian are in need of repair as originally designed according to God's purpose. We may seem to be in a broken down condition, but never forget that God is still working all things for good according to His purpose.

Now back to the model and serial numbers. What model are we exactly? What number is indelibly stamped upon our hearts as Christians that makes us all function identically? How is it that we are all the same as believers no matter the date we believed, the circumstance that brought us to salvation, or the location in which we reside?

We are all marked with one model number:

J-E-S-U-S

It is Jesus that marks us all as belonging to the identical model. He is the first fruit of all who believe. (1 Cor. 15:23) We are all designed after Him as His prototype and each of us is to function according to the purpose of the J-E-S-U-S model.

But where then is our individuality as believers? Are we all to walk lock step as one? Is there to be no variety among believers or among churches?

Again the purpose of God triumphs. He did not begin a process of designing us all according to the J-E-S-U-S model only to become bored with our mundane sameness.

God in His infinite wisdom makes each of us unique. As we roll off "the salvation assembly line", we are given a particular serial number if you please. I am totally different from you and you are uniquely designed to be just who you are in Christ.

The Creator performs this serial process by equipping each Christian with spiritual gifts that function uniquely in us but always with the purpose of God being fulfilled. We are able then to exist as individuals, but all bearing the model number of J-E-S-U-S stamped deeply upon our being.

The purpose of God is revealed in each J-E-S-U-S model through one of these functions:

1. We model the gospel of salvation.

2. We model surrender.

3. We model suffering.

4. We model reconciliation.

5. We model second-coming perseverance.

It is only fitting that Paul would mention the purpose of God in the last letter he wrote or at least the last of his writings that we have as a portion of our Bible. As Paul wrote from the confines of prison to his young protégé Timothy, he instructed him about God who is the One "who has saved us and called us with a holy calling, not according to our works, but according to His own purpose and grace which was given to us in Christ Jesus before time began..." (2 Timothy 1:9)

The word translated purpose here is the same that was used in Romans 8:28. It is the word *prosthesis*. It carries the idea of intention. A purpose expects an anticipated outcome and guides planned actions. This is exactly what God is doing in the life of the Christian.

MODELING THE GOSPEL OF SALVATION

God's intention is for us to model the gospel of salvation to the world in which we live at this very moment. This intention presupposes that the one modeling salvation has indeed been saved. Only a church made up of Christians (born again believers) can present the message of salvation.

Over and again as Paul addressed his letters to churches and individuals, he placed his words in careful order. He always listed the grace of God as a precedent to being at peace with God. For example, his first letter to the Thessalonians states, "Paul, Silvanus, and Timothy, to the church of the Thessalonians in God the Father and the Lord Jesus Christ: grace to you and peace from God our Father and the Lord Jesus Christ." (1 Thessalonians 1:1)

As the world peers into the Christian life, there needs to be a quick and ready demonstration of what our purpose is as believers. Without the experience of grace in our lives and the peace that comes from that grace, the world will lose interest and turn from the church.

It has been noted that the world turned to the church immediately after September 11, 2001. The terrorist's attack on the two towers of the World Trade Center drove many to the church with the hope of finding answers. Honestly, I think the world wanted to know what purpose was unfolding in these attacks.

Pundits came out of the woodwork with explanations. Blame was placed upon all sorts of causes, but ultimately the world wanted to know how God could let something like this happen. It seemed that almost instinctively people knew that all of this was according to some plan that was bigger than themselves.

They were right. If you believe that God's purpose was already in place prior to these attacks, then the attack was no surprise to God and ultimately could be used for good according to His purpose.

This leaves no reason to have to explain away God's part in the equation. ALL things are working together for good and are ALWAYS fulfilling His purpose.

The world turned to the church for answers, but found none. Since the church did not clearly understand its purpose and Christians could not respond to tragedy with the calm assurance of God's peace, the world simply looked somewhere else. Within weeks, church attendance was back to normal—if you could call pre-9/11 normal.

The church had lost its opportunity to model the message of salvation to a lost and searching world. It was not a matter of the church being occupied by unbelievers alone. There was the evidence that those who were believing had somehow been disconnected from the source of their power.

Any model of any sort that is powerless will never be able to perform its intended purpose. Unfortunately, this is the condition of the church today. We are fully created according to God's intended purpose, but we are unplugged from the power source.

Have you ever turned to a trouble-shooting section in an owner's manual to get some idea of the reason a machine won't function correctly? If you have, you probably came across this statement near the top the page:

MAKE SURE UNIT IS PLUGGED INTO AN ELECTRICAL SOURCE.

This statement is there for a reason. It is listed first in most cases for a reason also. It is the most common cause of malfunction. The model you own simply isn't designed to perform its function without power. Only an empowered church can present the message of salvation in such an impelling way that it simply cannot be ignored.

Once again, Paul addresses this matter in the beginning of one of his letters. Like the statement shown above is listed early in the trouble-shooting guide, Paul reminds the church at Thessalonica, "For our gospel did not come to you in word only, but also in power, and in the Holy Spirit and in much assurance, as you know what kind of men we were among you for your sake. (1 Thessalonians 1:5)

Paul makes it clear that understanding the label attached to the model is not enough. Until you plug it into a power source it can never fulfill its purpose. The gospel of salvation needs God's power source engaged through the plug of the Holy Spirit. Then the switch can be thrown with assurance as we live out our lives in the presence of others.

The world will see the message of the gospel modeled in tangible ways instead of trapped in the mystery of methodology.

The best example I have of this comes from my childhood. My father was a man of few words. When I needed correction as a boy, my dad would just clear his throat. I knew when I heard this that he meant business. I needed to respond immediately, because that harrumph was backed up with power.

Children today listen as parents count to three or use some other tactic to persuade performance. All that is needed is a demonstration of power.

Now lest you think that I was beaten as a child, the opposite is actually true. Because I recognized and respected the power behind the words, I needed fewer demonstrations of that power.

Be like the Apostle Paul. Let others know what manner of person you are among them as you model the work of salvation. The power of that salvation will be demonstrated and the world will clearly see God's purpose at work in your life.

MODELING SURRENDER TO A LOST WORLD

The concept of surrender does not come easily to most people; especially to those who consider themselves free. This, of course, includes all who dwell in the home of the free and the land of the brave.

Unfortunately, this American ideal of freedom has been brought with full force into the church. This has prompted Christians to take on a belief of spiritual independence and declare as such a glorified bill of rights. This is totally contrary to our purpose of modeling surrender to the world.

In the face of all of our perceived rights as believers we must deal forthrightly with Paul's teaching about our salvation and the relationship that we now have with God. In his letter to the Romans, Paul declared us to be slaves. Not only slaves in our relationship to God, but that we were slaves before our salvation also. Slaves, as it were, to sin.

"But now having been set free from sin, and having become slaves of God, you have your fruit to holiness, and the end, everlasting life." (Romans 6:22)

Paul makes it clear that our surrender to God makes us His slaves. This causes some to have an immediate repulsive reaction. Some are convinced that turning to God for salvation means a surrender of their rights.

You are correct in assuming that a relationship with God, i.e., becoming a Christian, means that rights will be surrendered. Paul does not hide this fact from us and says so in the beginning of this verse as he makes plain the essence of Christianity: we become slaves to God.

We were already slaves—slaves to sin. Amazingly, we were slaves and in that slavery were deceived into believing that we were free to do as we pleased. In reality, we could do nothing except obey the demands that sin placed upon our lives. We, thinking that our rights were intact, had no privilege of freedom. The right to do right was not ours. Because of sin, we could only do wrong. (Romans 7)

Jesus comes to make us free in the midst of our surrender. He said to those who believed in Him, "If you abide in My word, you are My disciples indeed. And you shall know the truth, and the truth shall make you free." (John 8:31-32)

The truth is that Jesus is the truth. So he declared to his disciples in John 14:6: "I am the way, the truth, and the life." He alone can be the Master of our lives. He is the One to who we must surrender as Lord.

It is in this moment of surrender that we find true freedom and as Paul tells us above in the verse from Romans, "you have your fruit to holiness, and the end, everlasting life."

Few who are living today and might read these words have a very good understanding of surrender. The concept of surrender simply hasn't been modeled well to this generation. We live in a world that says everyone has a right to have things their way. Personal rights trump all other beliefs.

Many believe that having it your way is the only way. From having your hamburger prepared any way you want, people have started defining what should be called sin. Everything becomes a matter of personal preference. The consensus is that anyone who dares ask someone to surrender their beliefs to the wisdom of God's word is a bigot at best and a potential slave master at worst.

This generation has never seen an actual victory declared at the end of a war. The last time outright victory was declared and unconditional surrender was demanded occurred at the end of World War II.

Since that time all of the wars and conflicts that have been engaged by the United States have concluded in a stalemate. New lines are drawn and enemies are kept apart by demilitarized zones, but there is no unconditional surrender.

For unconditional surrender to be demanded a victor must be declared. Without a victor no one has any reason to surrender and that is where we find many who claim the name of Christ.

I am afraid that many today have simply decided to cease fighting and lay down their resistance. Thinking that God will bargain with them for a cease fire, they have formed a spiritual DMZ. A no-man's-land now exists between them and God. They are happy to stay on their side of the border and are quite content for God to stay on His side also.

This scenario is simply not biblical, however. God is not interested in our peace keeping plans. His purpose was to send His only Son into the battle against sin. That battle was won on Calvary Hill. The last shot was fired from hell into the hands, feet, and side of Jesus and he died there declaring that all was finished.

But wait! This doesn't appear to be victory. Jesus seemed to be vanquished and all appeared to be lost. Hell, sin, and the grave had declared a defeat to God's purpose.

But wait again! Three days later Christ arose! He had beaten back hell. He had paid the price for sin. He had left the grave empty of its claim over mankind. He had done it all through surrender to His Father's will.

This is what we learn from Paul's letter to the Philippians. "Let this mind be in you which was also in Christ Jesus, who, being in the form of God, did not consider it robbery to be equal with God, but made Himself of no reputation, taking the form of a bondservant, and coming in the likeness of men. And being found in appearance as a man, He humbled Himself and became obedient to the point of death, even the death of the cross." (Philippians 2:5-8)

There's the truth of God's purpose unfolding before us. Jesus set the example for our surrender as He became a willing bondservant (slave) and was obedient to the point of death.

This is the model of surrender that is part of God's purpose for your life. As Christ was our example of surrender so we should be offering our daily lives as an example of surrender to a world that will never understand unless we live it out before them.

May your life and mine be marked by unconditional surrender. For you see, unless you are surrendered unconditionally, you are not surrendered at all!

Let the testimony of the Thessalonians be yours today: "And you became followers of us and of the Lord, having received the word in much affliction, with joy of the Holy Spirit, so that you became examples to all in Macedonia and Achaia who believe. For from you the word of the Lord has sounded forth, not only in Macedonia and Achaia, but also in every place. Your faith toward God has gone out, so that we do not need to say anything. For they themselves declare concerning us what manner of entry we had to you, and how you turned to God from idols to serve the living and true God, and to wait for His Son from heaven, whom He raised from the dead, even Jesus who delivers us from the wrath to come." (1 Thessalonians 1:6-10)

MODELING SUFFERING TO A LOST WORLD

As God's purpose unfolds it becomes clear very quickly that His purpose does not always exist in the sunshine. We have all experienced the truth that bad things happen to good people. Is this a flaw in God's designing? Should He adjust His purpose so that the church and the Christian can avoid the pitfalls of life? What can God hope to accomplish in allowing His plans to include suffering?

All of these are good questions. All are questions that you may have asked at some time in your life. They are also questions that are not usually answered to our satisfaction.

Here is the one thing I have noted about suffering: Christian suffering does not differ from that which the world experiences. Pain is pain; loss is loss; grief is grief. It matters not that you are born-again. Suffering does not come in degrees that are comparable to one's walk with Christ.

It just comes...

The difference that exists is the reaction the Christian has to suffering when compared to the world's reaction. The believer reacts based on the assurance that everything is working according to God's purpose and because of this God intends good to come from the suffering.

As Paul recounted the suffering he had endured he stated it this way, "But we have this treasure in earthen vessels, that the excellence of the power may be of God and not of us. We are hard-pressed on every side, yet not crushed; we are perplexed, but not in despair; persecuted, but not forsaken; struck down, but not destroyed—" (2 Corinthians 4:7-9)

Remember earlier when the power was discussed. Here it is again. As only an empowered church can present the message of salvation, a demonstration of suffering also must be accompanied by power. This is the key to a correct reaction when suffering comes to us as it surely will.

God has entrusted us with the treasure of His salvation message as it is found in Jesus Christ. The shining light of that treasure is hidden inside every Christian. We did not place it there of our own accord and we cannot simply take it out for display upon our own whim.

We are unconditionally surrendered property. Our lives belong to the Master and are to be used at His discretion. It is at His will that the light of the gospel shines forth in our lives. That light shines best in times of dark suffering.

We are just earthen vessels. We are like the clay pitchers that held the torches of Gideon's army (Judges 7:15-22). Gideon ordered his soldiers to hide their lights inside the earthen vessels until the appointed moment. Then at his word, they were to break the pitchers and let the light shine in the darkness. An army of 300 routed the entire Syrian encampment.

Our lives are like the clay pitchers of Gideon's day. They had no mind of their own. These pitchers were under the control of Gideon's men. It was up to the men to break them at the right time. There would be no restoration of the pitchers or a return to their former use.

Under the authority of another, they were to be destroyed so God's power could be released upon the Syrians. We, like the pitchers of Gideon's army, are just earthen vessels that need to be cracked open before the power of God's glory can shine. That cracking sometimes takes suffering.

How is it possible to react with such calm assurance in the face of irreparable suffering? It can only be done when you consider yourself already dead. You see, the ultimate suffering comes in the form of martyrdom.

This is why Paul continued in his discourse to the Corinthians: "always carrying about in the body the dying of the Lord Jesus, that the life of Jesus also may be manifested in our body. For we who live are always delivered to death for Jesus' sake, that the life of Jesus also may be manifested in our mortal flesh. So then death is working in us, but life in you." (2 Corinthians 4:1-12)

Paul went on to say to the Galatians, "I have been crucified with Christ; it is no longer I who live, but Christ lives in me; and the life which I now live in the flesh I live by faith in the Son of God, who loved me and gave Himself for me." (Galatians 2:20)

Clearly, Paul could face all of the suffering that he details in several of his letters to churches and individuals, because he had already reckoned himself dead. Lest this sounds a bit morbid, a better understanding of martyrdom is needed.

There are two distinct types of martyrs. You will find evident throughout history both the Christian martyr and the religious martyr.

I use the word Christian here to identify the born-again believer only. I use the word religious in a very broad sense. This person may be martyred for many reasons which may be religious, but particularly, martyrdom occurs as a result of some avid belief. That belief bears ideals that attain to the height of religious fervor and fanaticism.

The distinction in these two is thus noted: Where the religious martyr lives to die, the Christian martyr dies in order to live.

Jimmy Draper speaking of the original meaning of martyrdom said, "The death of Christians did not make them martyrs; it only revealed them to be martyrs. They were martyrs long before they gave up their lives!"

Leighton Ford noted in his book, One Way to Change the World, "What then is a martyr? He is a confessor. A martyr is one who is first convinced of a truth, and then yields his life to the claims of the truth of which he is convinced, and who, therefore, is changed by the truth which he believes, and to which he had yielded himself...A martyr is a specimen, an evidence, a sample, a credential, a proof, a witness."

God breaks us open through suffering so we can present to the world a model for suffering. As Ford said we are specimens, evidences, samples, credentials, proofs, and witnesses of God using suffering to demonstrate the truth of His power to make good His purpose!

Not that I have attained anywhere close to the level of the Apostle Paul's faith in this matter, but I have been given a personal and close-up view of suffering and the proper response to it. This opportunity came through the diagnosis of Lou Gehrig's Disease.

My first wife, Kay, was diagnosed with this disease on her birthday in 2008. Neither she nor I had any misconceptions about the doctor's evaluation of her condition. Her father, aunt, and cousin had all succumbed to the same disease. We knew that it was a death sentence.

Kay's reaction to this news of forthcoming suffering was one that I am not sure I could produce. Only the grace of God could have bestowed such a response in the face of her earthen vessel being shattered.

The evidence of her willingness to suffer to the point of death came quickly after the diagnosis of ALS or Lou Gehrig's Disease. She was willing to be a specimen, an evidence, a sample, a credential, a proof, and a witness.

As we sat in our vehicle in the parking lot of the doctor's office, she said, "Thank God it's me and not one of my brothers or sisters." Simple. To the point. Without emotional distress, she thought of her brothers and sisters who did not know Christ as Lord and Savior. Kay was one of eleven siblings.

The next opportunity to let the light shine came in the living room of our home. We had summoned our four children and their spouses to gather there for the purpose of disclosing the results of the visit to the doctors.

I struggled for words. Here I was, the husband, the father, and yes, the preacher and I had no words. But Kay did. It was her struggle and her suffering. By God's grace it was her time to speak the words of a martyr.

After a few moments of attempting to break the bad news to our children she gave two simple, yet profound statements that embody the model of suffering to a lost world.

1. I'm not angry with God and I don't want you to be.
2. If God does nothing more for me, He has done enough.

And that, my friend, is a true model of suffering!

MODELING RECONCILATION

If then the world is really looking for proof of the Christian life and our purpose in being a Christian is to provide an evidence of that proof as we live out God's purpose, how exactly can we perform this duty that has been thrust upon us?

It begins in each of the three ways that I have already mentioned. We are to model the gospel of salvation to a lost world. We are to model surrender to the world so they might be made free. We are to model suffering in such a way that those around us can clearly see that all things really do work together for good to those who are called.

These steps bring us to the fourth concept that we are to model to those we encounter on our life's journey. Our purpose is to present to the world the model of reconciliation.

Another quote from Leighton Ford speaks to the evidence of reconciliation and the importance of living our lives as ministers of reconciliation. "We are the proof of these things. We say Jesus is risen from the dead. We say the risen Christ is the self-same Christ who was crucified. We say this Christ is exalted by God…How are we going to prove these things? We are evidences. We prove the accuracy of our doctrine by the transformation of our lives…Go back and think of us as we were, and behold us as we are."

Ford hits the nail on the head. We are the models of reconciliation to God, because we ourselves have been reconciled. This is what the Apostle Paul makes clear in his second letter to the Corinthian church.

"Therefore, if anyone is in Christ, he is a new creation; old things have passed away; behold, all things have become new. Now all things are of God, who has reconciled us to Himself through Jesus Christ, and has given us the ministry of reconciliation, that is, that God was in Christ reconciling the world to Himself, not imputing their trespasses to them, and has committed to us the word of reconciliation." (2 Corinthians 5:17-20)

We are models of reconciliation through the presentation of changed lives. People may try to deny the validity of the Bible. They may challenge the account of creation. They may scoff at the miracles. Charges may be levied against the integrity of the church. But no one can deny a changed life!

As Ford said, "We are evidences. We prove the accuracy of our doctrine by the transformation of our lives…Go back and think of us as we were, and behold us as we are."

The very fact that we have been changed gives us a message to declare openly to the world in which we live. We have the good news of the gospel beating in our breasts. We should have the fire of Jeremiah in our bones who said after much ridicule and abuse, "'I will not make mention of Him, nor speak anymore in His name.' But His word was in my heart like a burning fire shut up in my bones; I was weary of holding it back, and I could not." (Jeremiah 20:9)

Our testimonies, though varied, will have one common thread. There will be an unnatural power that is evident. It will be undeniable to those who hear us speak of Christ that we once were calculated and self-reliant, but now are living surrendered lives as servants of the living Lord.

A changed life presents a message of hope because we can confidently proclaim that old things are passed away and all things have become new for us. The Christian is the proof of God's purpose being realized daily in a life that has been reconciled to God.

Reconciliation is an act that brings about mutual change. Since God does not change in His character (Malachi 3:6), then reconciliation must be a change of our character that produces a change in our relationship to God.

There is in the act of reconciling a cessation of hostilities. We literally were enemies of God before we became Christians. That leads us back to our second model of surrender—unconditional surrender.

God is not going to change, because He cannot. He, therefore, has provided a way for the necessary change to take place through an act of reconciliation. This act requires God on His part to make restitution for wrongs committed (sins) by the offending party. Just as God cannot change, mankind does not have the capacity to make right all that is wrong in their relationship with God.

Through the sacrifice of Jesus, the atonement is accomplished and our war with God ends with our total surrender under His unconditional terms. We are made to be at one with God, that is, we are reconciled. In essence, that act defines atonement. It is at-one-ment!

As God's purpose unfolds through reconciling us to Himself, He then bestows upon each Christian the responsibility of modeling reconciliation to others. He does this in two distinct ways.

First, God has given Christians the ministry of reconciliation. We are to serve God by serving others. The word ministry comes from the same word in the original manuscripts from which we derive our English word deacon.

Our greatest opportunity to model reconciliation and to fulfil God's purpose in saving us is to serve one another. This can be seen with no more clarity than in those final moments before Jesus went to Calvary.

In the Upper Room, as Jesus gave final instructions to the disciples and they fellowshipped in what we call the Last Supper, an amazing picture of servanthood unfolded in their midst.

"And supper being ended…Jesus, knowing that the Father had given all things into His hands, and that He had come from God and was going to God, rose from supper and laid aside His garments, took a towel and girded Himself. After that, He poured water into a basin and began to wash the disciples' feet, and to wipe them with the towel with which He was girded." (John 13:2-5)

You may remember that Peter wanted to deny this foot washing on Jesus' part. Jesus told Peter and by inference all of the disciples that they did not presently understand what he was demonstrating, but they would soon enough.

As the scene closes Jesus asked them, "'Do you know what I have done to you?'"

He went on to say, "'You call Me Teacher and Lord, and you say well, for so I am. If I then, your Lord and Teacher, have washed your feet, you also ought to wash one another's feet. For I have given you an example, that you should do as I have done to you. Most assuredly, I say to you, a servant is not greater than his master; nor is he who is sent greater than he who sent him. If you know these things, blessed are you if you do them.'" (John 13:12-17)

Here is the greatest picture you can find of God's purpose for us as Christians. Jesus modeled for us in this one act that we could be washed from our sins, that we were to exhibit to the world an attitude of service as we take on the role of the lowest servant, that suffering for His name will sometimes be at the feet of others, and that the most blessed ministry we can have in reconciliation is by serving others.

Second, God has given us the word of reconciliation. The idea here is that of full representation to the world as an ambassador of God.

Ambassadors act with full authority from their country and its leader. They serve as such with full credentials or as we have already discussed: proof.

An ambassador can speak on behalf of those who have appointed him. His words are to be received as though the king who sent him were speaking the words himself.

We have a word from God. Literally, we have the logo of God. Our word logo is derived from the same Greek term. A logo is a clearly identifiable mark, symbol, or insignia that lets someone know readily what product or power resides behind such logo.

One example of this is the American flag. It is clearly recognizable around the world. When it is presented, no one doubts the power and full force that stands behind it.

For the Christian, the word of reconciliation resides in our very name. Paul declared in verse 19 from above, "that God was in Christ reconciling the world to Himself."

When we are bold enough to claim the name of Christ, we need to be bold enough to declare that we are here fulfilling God's purpose as we model reconciliation.

MODELING SECOND-COMING PERSEVERANCE

This brings us to the last point I will make about the church and Christians modeling the purpose of God. As stated before, I do not assume that these five models are inclusive of all the ways we can model God's purpose for us.

These five seem to me to be the most prevalent and most easily recognizable. They may be the most easy to live out on a daily basis, but seeing their lack of display in so many Christians makes me wonder why they are missing in so many lives.

We should especially be desirous of modeling the purpose of God in light of the fact that these are clearly the last days. I know you must be thinking, "Last days? Haven't preachers and teachers been talking about the last days forever?"

Yes, they have, but I can assure you that as you read this we are closer to the second coming of Jesus than we have ever been before! As a matter of fact, you may not be able to finish this book due to His appearing and that's perfectly fine with me. I only pray that you are ready for His coming!

Doubting His coming is no new phenomenon. Peter wrote in the first few decades after Christ's ascension, "knowing this first: that scoffers will come in the last days, walking according to their own lusts, and saying, "Where is the promise of His coming? For since the fathers fell asleep, all things continue as they were from the beginning of creation." (2 Peter 3:3-4)

Our lives as Christians should be lived in stark contrast to those who are doubters. We will never live in a time without doubters, but we can be the model of perseverance based on the assurance of His coming. Peter in his last epistle tells his readers that he is writing this letter to "stir up your pure minds by way of reminder." (2 Peter 3:1)

Doubt has its root in the elapsing of time. As mere mortals we cannot wrap ourselves up tightly enough to understand the concept of time in light of eternity.

Remember, I began this book by attempting to take you back to the beginning, because we need such points in time to get a proper understanding of things. Truthfully, though, I may have complicated this last point by doing so. As Christians, we are to persevere until the end without knowing when the end is and we do so not knowing exactly where it all began.

Confused? Doubting? Don't be! Peter puts it all in perspective with this verse: "But, beloved, do not forget this one thing, that with the Lord one day is as a thousand years, and a thousand years as one day." (2 Peter 3:8)

Let's assume for just a moment that this old earth and all that was created is about 6000 years old. (This is really what I believe, but that's a discussion for another book and time, no pun intended!) If all that was created is in the concluding stages of 6000 years and if each 1000 years is like a day to God, then we are nearing the 7000th year.

This would mean that we are approaching a day of rest similar to when God had concluded all of His work and rested. (Genesis 2:2) We, therefore, can persevere in the face of the doubters, because we know how God calculates time!

Peter goes on to say that because all that now is will soon be no more, we ought to be living lives that model the holiness of God. "Therefore, since all these things will be dissolved, what manner of persons ought you to be in holy conduct and godliness…" (2 Peter 3:11)

Do you see the J-E-S-U-S model? We are to lives our lives according to our model—**Jesus!**

Not only will your life be lived in contrast to doubters, it will be lived out in continuing dispersion. God's purpose will be fulfilled wherever you live. His purpose is not restrained by geography, but enhanced as He empowers you to be His witness (martyr).

Just before Jesus ascended into heaven he told his disciples, "But you shall receive power when the Holy Spirit has come upon you; and you shall be witnesses to Me in Jerusalem, and in all Judea and Samaria, and to the end of the earth.'" (Acts 1:8)

Jesus left those disciples with God's purpose for their lives. It remains the purpose of all Christians to this day! Now go forth and model Jesus to a lost and dying world until the very end of your time!

You've been empowered!

Mileposts

From where does the idea of purpose come and why does it demand a creator that exceeds the restraint of time?

_____

_____

_____

_____

How does God's purpose at work in your life guarantee that all things will work for good?

_____

_____

_____

_____

List the five ways which we can model God's purpose and give one key verse that relates to each model.

_____

_____

_____

_____

How important is it that the Christian is empowered to live out the J-E-S-U-S model?

_____

_____

_____

_____

Chapter Four

THE PASSION

Choosing to introduce the idea of passion as an evidence for the Christian life left me with a bit of a pause. The word passion can be used in many ways. Some of them have a very negative connotation and lead down a path that no Christian should go.

When passion is left uncontrolled in our flesh it can destroy us, but when we lose our passion for the things of God, we become dull to His design as it works itself out in our lives and in the world around us.

Passion ebbs and flows. Several words come to mind that describe the power of passion as it is released. Words such as fervor, zeal, ardent love, and boundless enthusiasm are just a few that can serve as synonyms.

We are greatly affected in our passion by the price demanded of it. Years ago I saw a cartoon strip in the Sunday paper on Mother's Day.

It was one of the many that had been written by Ernie Bushmiller in his famous *Nancy* series. Nancy was shown in a department store as she shopped for a Mother's Day gift. Each scene depicted her asking the clerk for a more and more expensive bottle of perfume to consider as her mother's gift.

She finally settle upon a bottle that cost several hundred dollars. At this point she told the clerk, "That's it!" "That's the one I want!" She then told the clerk that she wanted 50 cents worth of this most exquisite perfume!

Her passion for her mother was tempered by her ability to pay the cost required. Her heart was in the right place, but her resources were limited.

So it is with many of us when it comes to fulfilling a call to a passionate evidence for our claim to Christianity. Until you understand that the passion required of us has no cost, nor could it ever be measured in mere dollars, you might assume that attempting a passionate Christian life is futile.

Yes, passion ebbs and flows. It can be restricted by our own lack of resources, but it can also be dampened by the circumstances that come our way. The following account details a portion of Robertson McQuilkin's struggle to maintain his passion for the things of God.

R.J. Morgan in *Nelson's Complete Book of Stories, Illustrations, and Quotes* details the testimony of Robertson McQuilkin, former president of Columbia International University of Columbia, South Carolina, as he recalls a time when the circumstances of his life nearly extinguished his passion.

"Life was heavy on me. My dearest friend and intimate companion, my delightful wife Muriel, was slipping away, one painful loss at a time, as Alzheimer's disease ravaged her brain. Just as the full impact of what was happening to us hit home, the life of Bob, our eldest son, was snuffed out in a diving accident.

Two years later, to care for Muriel, I left my life work at its peak. I was numb. Not bitter, let alone angry. Why should I be? That's the way life is, life in a broken world. But the *passion* in my love for God had evaporated, leaving a residue of resignation where once had been vibrant faith.

I knew that I was in deep trouble, and I did the only thing I knew to do—I went away to a mountain hideaway for prayer and fasting. It took about twenty-four hours to shake free of preoccupation with my own wounds and to focus on the excellencies of God. As I did, slowly love began to be rekindled. And with love came joy.

I wrote God a love letter, naming forty-one of his marvelous gifts to me, spotlighting eleven of his grandest acts in history, and exulting in ten of his characteristics that exceed my imagination. Surely he enjoyed my gratitude—who doesn't appreciate gratitude?

But I discovered something else. Something happened to me. I call it the reflex action of thanksgiving. My love flamed up from the dying embers, and my spirit soared. I discovered that ingratitude impoverishes—but that a heavy heart lifts on the wings of praise." [*emphasis mine*]

McQuilkin's story is so much like many of yours. The names may be changed, the disease may track a different path, the response may be convoluted a bit, but in the end passion takes a hit. We lose our ability to love God and with that loss goes one of the evidences for our Christian claim. The world stands ready in the shadows to ask the age old question, "Where is your God now?" (Psalm 42:10)

How exactly are we to live out this life of passion? How can we maintain a high level of passion? Is there a way to make smooth some of the mountaintops and raise some of the valleys as we journey through life? I hope to answer these questions and others that might have already popped up in your mind.

Passion in the Christian life can be demonstrated in four distinct ways. These four ways are not inclusive, but I believe that all other passionate responses in the Christian life will be derivatives of these four processes.

Consider this concept as we begin to unfold the evidence of passion. The ultimate passion of the church and the Christian is similar to the passion that a bride has for her bridegroom. This level of passion is shown in tangible ways.

This is no shallow, internalized passion. The passion of the bride is demonstrated in an open proclamation of her love for the bridegroom. This is the intensity of which I speak when considering the evidence of passion.

When Jesus revealed His plan for the church and for the Christians who would be called out, he asked a question that demonstrated the need for a passionate answer. You can find the details of this story in Matthew's gospel.

Jesus had taken His disciples to the northern reaches of Israel. Here in the province of Dan, they visited Caesarea Phillipi. This area had become a religious mecca. Thousands came here to pray and offer sacrifices to their gods.

In the alcoves that were carved into the cliff face, statues of these gods were placed and homage was offered to them all. This area was the birthplace of pantheism. This is a belief that God is in all things tangible. Because of this need for a tangible source of God's existence and since God was in all things that exist, this religious system denies a personal God who can be related to with passion.

Matthew tells us, When Jesus came into the region of Caesarea Philippi, He asked His disciples, saying, "Who do men say that I, the Son of Man, am?"

So they said, "Some say John the Baptist, some Elijah, and others Jeremiah or one of the prophets."

He said to them, "But who do you say that I am?"

Simon Peter answered and said, "You are the Christ, the Son of the living God."

Jesus answered and said to him, "Blessed are you, Simon Bar-Jonah, for flesh and blood has not revealed this to you, but My Father who is in heaven." (Matthew 16:13-17)

This world into which Jesus posed the question of His identity is very similar to our world today. Religion was hostile to the concepts of Christianity and the remainder of the folks were just looking for a show to entertain themselves as they toiled under Roman rule.

It was under these circumstances that Jesus narrowed the focus from mere hearsay to fact. From a generic question about what others had to say, he demanded a response from the disciples based on what they knew of Him.

He was moving them from a shallow response based on the latest report from the crowds, to a passionate answer based on their own personal belief. The answer, however, did not come from the limited resources of a human heart. It came from heaven itself. It was given from God Himself.

Like Nancy buying expensive perfume in tiny quantities, the best we can do in demonstrating our passion is join in with the most popular definition of passion as devised by nominal followers of Christ. It is when we get our passion from above that we are most ready to proclaim with fervor, zeal, ardent love, and boundless enthusiasm, ""You are the Christ, the Son of the living God." (Matthew 16:16)

Our Passion Should Be For the Glory of God

Passion should be a simple by-product of the grace of God at work in our lives. Because we are the recipients of grace, we can be passionate as a direct response to that grace working in us. When passion begins to flow from a grace-touched life, God alone receives the glory.

This is no hyper-religious outburst. There is no ecstatic language spoken. No one is doing back flips over the pews. The Christian shows evidence of being touched by grace in living a passionate life to the glory of God. In essence, worth is attributed to God. Or as we like to say, we worship Him.

We get our term worship from the Old English. The word worship is a shortened form of worth-ship. We attribute worth to that which should receive our passionate response. One simply cannot worship dispassionately.

This worship translates into a lifestyle of passion. From this everyday living the Christian walks worthy of God in all details of life. In doing so, this person establishes a further evidence for a claim to the title of Christian. Paul encouraged the church at Thessalonica to walk this way as he said, "...you know how we exhorted, and comforted, and charged every one of you, as a father does his own children, that you would walk worthy of God who calls you into His own kingdom and glory. (1 Thessalonians 2:11-12)

To exhibit passion in the Christian life is not an element that is added on as a secondary development. Passion flows out of the reality that we have been called into a living relationship with the God of the universe through His Son, Jesus Christ.

That calling prompts a passionate response which in turn produces a worthy walk that glorifies God. Passion is drawn out of such a relationship. There is no way to contain it. It must flow freely and to restrain it is impossible.

I can still remember during my years in the pastorate those occasions when someone would receive Christ as Lord and Savior. Often there would be a spontaneous burst of passionate response. It took on many forms from quiet crying to shouts of praise, but it was undeniable that some levee had broken in the heart. From this breach poured out all of the passionate response to the working of grace in a life that had been earlier condemned.

Unfortunately, I also remember the response of some folks to such outburst. One of the most common fell somewhere along these lines. "Well, I'm happy for their decision, but they will get over it soon enough and settle down."

God help us to never settle down so much that we lose our passion. When that day comes then one of the primary evidences of our Christianity is irreparably harmed. Settling down is just not possible when it comes to a vibrant, ever-flowing passion.

Is this all there is to passion? Is God glorified only by some passionate response? Is there a more tangible way in which our passion can be demonstrated and thereby our witness as a Christian be proven?

The answers to these questions are simple:

No!
No!
&
Yes!

Passion is so much more than some emotional response. Matthew records the words of Jesus as He spoke from the Mount of Beatitudes, "You are the light of the world. A city that is set on a hill cannot be hidden. Nor do they light a lamp and put it under a basket, but on a lampstand, and it gives light to all who are in the house. Let your light so shine before men, that they may see your good works and glorify your Father in heaven." (Matthew 5:14-16)

Like a brightly burning light our passion will be clearly seen by the world. When we are truly passionate there is no hiding it. Our demonstration of passion will be seen as a city lights up a hillside in the dark of night.

Here again, the result of passion is for the glory of God alone. Our passion may be attributed to us as we respond to God's grace, but those who look to us as Christians should look beyond our meager attempts and give all glory to our Father in heaven.

The moment others give praise to us for our devotion we cease to be lights of passion and this evidence of being a Christian is extinguished. As the children's song says, "This little light of mine, I'm gonna let it shine."

Our Passion Should Be For the Guidebook of Scripture

You cannot really discuss the concept of passion without considering the element of love. You cannot understand correctly the concept of love unless you look to the greatest love letter that has ever been written: the Bible.

In this one book God has openly displayed his passionate love for mankind. From the opening pages of the Bible when God searches for Adam and Eve after the great fall to the supreme sacrifice of His own Son on the cross to pay for that original sin, we see God's love being poured out to us.

Yes, you can love God also. But our love is only in response to Him first loving us. "In this is love, not that we loved God, but that He loved us and sent His Son to be the propitiation for our sins." (1 John 4:10) We need to find some guide that will help us know how to best demonstrate our passion for this One who has loved us so deeply and unselfishly.

That guidebook is the Bible. In the pages of this book, we find one character after another that loved God supremely. Abraham, the friend of God, loved God enough to leave his homeland and go to a country that God would only reveal after he had arrived. David had a deep passion for God that pours out in the lines of each hymn recorded in the book of Psalms.

Prophets both minor and major followed his commands explicitly to their own detriment and sometimes to their death. Disciples took sharp detours in their paths at the simple command of, "Follow me!"

Men like Paul left their heritage, their religion, and their families behind to follow Jesus by faith and declare openly their love for God. John, who is noted as the beloved disciple, spent his final years on this earth exiled to an island, but in doing so saw the grandest vision yet of the resurrected Christ.

All of these left behind for us a history of passionate following of the God of glory and His Son, Jesus Christ. Paul declared to the Corinthians that all of these things were written for our example. (1 Corinthians 10:11) With these character studies (both good and bad), we can learn how to be passionate as Christians.

The church can show her love for the One who gave Himself for her as the world sees love defined openly in the believers. "By this all will know that you are My disciples, if you have love for one another." (John 13:35) Only as the guidebook of Scripture is believed to be inerrant and infallible will it serve as a standard for our zeal and ardent love for God. Are you clearly defined as Christian? Is there unmistakable evidence of your passion as seen in your boundless enthusiasm for the things of God and your love for other Christian brothers and sisters?

Sadly, it is possible to be a Christian and your passion to be discarded. When you no longer look to the guidebook of Scripture as a vital part of your daily walk with Jesus, you soon turn your attention toward lesser affections.

This was the charge that was brought against the church at Laodicea. These Christians had set very high standards for themselves. They were noted for hating evil, working hard, being patient, persevering in the face of trials, and not becoming weary in well doing. But with all of these positives, they had become dispassionate.

As Jesus walked in their midst he declared through John's prophecy in the last book of the Bible, "Nevertheless I have this against you, that you have left your first love." (Revelation 2:4) They had not lost their love. They simply had left it. Like a piece of baggage laid aside carelessly, they had put down the very evidence of their Christianity and walked away from it. They had left their first love—their passion!

To give the Laodiceans a little slack here might be appropriate. They had been careless in their love for Christ, but they did not have the history of God's workings at their disposal. They had no big, black Bibles to carry to church. Nor did they have massive translations of scripture and matching commentaries in easily searchable electronic format attached to their hips in the form of the latest storage device.

They might have had some small excuse, but you and I do not. We can read God's love letter any time of any day. We can peruse it's pages with ease and here in America without danger of repercussion. But we do not! And that is the real shame for the church today. We are more accountable than the Laodecians ever were.

You see it is scripture that keeps us fully aware of how we can properly demonstrate our passion for God. Without this guidebook, each of us could simply devise our own definition and be happy with ourselves as we love according to our own definition. But this is not possible, because we cannot fully understand love or its demonstration in passion until we seek the standard of the guidebook.

Jesus said, "If you love Me, keep My commandments." (John 14:5) He went on to ask, "But why do you call me, 'Lord, Lord,' and not do the things which I say?" (Luke 6:46)

It is made perfectly plain that the guidebook of scripture is the standard for our passion. Not only the standard for our passion, but it should cause us to be passionate for the book itself. It contains the words of life (Psalm 119:50).

After setting high standards that required His followers to eat of His flesh and drink of His blood, many followed Jesus no longer. He then turned to His disciples as recorded by John and asked a question that tested the depth of their passion. "Do you also want to go away?" (John 6:67)

Peter spoke for the group, "Lord, to whom shall we go? You have the words of eternal life." (John 6:68)

John MacArthur in *The Master's Plan for the Church* speaks of a painting in the cathedral of Lübeck, Germany, titled "The Lament of Jesus Christ Against the Ungrateful World." The associated text located in the painting reads,

> You call Me master, and obey Me not;
> You call Me light, and see Me not;
> You call Me the way, and walk Me not;
> You call Me life, and live Me not;
> You call Me wise, and follow Me not;
> You call Me fair, and love Me not;
> You call Me rich, and ask Me not;
> You call Me eternal, and seek Me not.
> If I condemn thee, blame Me not.

Indeed, these words ring true today when so many have left their first love and their passion has waned. No longer are sung the words of the old hymn written by Frederick Whitfield , "O how I love Jesus, O how I love Jesus, O how I love Jesus, because he first loved me!"

Passion can never be simulated, especially when it comes to the love one has for the guidebook of scripture. MacArthur goes on to recount a story told about an old pastor who had been forced to retire because years of preaching had caused his voice to crack.

The pastor was a humble man, but he was invited to a high–society luncheon by a friend. The person heading up the luncheon requested a famous actor who was present to recite something for the guests. Agreeing to do so, he asked if anyone had a specific request. The old pastor thought for a moment and said, "How about the Twenty–Third Psalm?"

The actor replied, "That's an unusual request, but I happen to know it. I'll do it on one condition, though: you recite it after me."

The old pastor hadn't bargained for that, but for the sake of the Lord, he agreed to follow the renowned actor.

The actor stood up and recited the Twenty–Third Psalm with the great intonation of his lyrical voice. When he finished, everyone applauded.

The old pastor then stood up and recited the psalm in his humble way with a soft-spoken crackling voice. When he was done, there was not a dry eye in the room.

Sensing the emotion of the moment, the actor stood up and said, "You clapped for me, but you wept for him. The difference is obvious: I know the psalm, but he knows the Shepherd."

Therein is the key to our passion for the guidebook of scripture. We must have a living relationship with the Shepherd first and then a love for His word.

Our Passion Is The Guarantee of Holiness

Holiness is not very often a topic that generates deep interest. It is an attribute that we reserve for God and God alone. We would prefer not to think too much about actually being holy. Perhaps we imagine that it will just go away if we don't talk about it.

There was a time that the favorite verse that most people would quote was John 3:16. Even in a tight spot someone could get most of this verse right when recalled from memory. Today another verse has taken its place as the most recalled. "Judge not, that you be not judged." (Matthew 7:1)

Why is it that we have left the infamous verse about receiving eternal life for one that speaks about judging? Could it be that this verse is being used as a cover for our lack of holiness?

God has made it very plain as to what part holiness plays in the Christian life. As a matter of fact, He states it as a clear command, "but as He who called you is holy, you also be holy in all your conduct, because it is written, 'Be holy, for I am holy.'" (1 Peter 1:15-16) We are to **BE** just as He **IS**.

This call to holiness is not an afterthought of God. It is part and parcel to His purpose. It began at the very point that He chose us as His own. So Paul tells the Ephesians, "…just as He chose us in Him before the foundation of the world, that we should be holy and without blame before Him in love…(Ephesians 1:4)

Holiness is not an option for the Christian. It is not a special condition that settles upon those who are somehow more deeply dedicated than others. It is a primary characteristic of the Christian life. Our passion demands holiness and our holiness guarantees that we will be passionate in our journey as a Christian.

It is after this word on holiness that is expected to be exhibited in the Christian life, that we hear Peter's remarks on how judging fits into the equation. "And if you call on the Father, who without partiality judges according to each one's work, conduct yourselves throughout the time of your stay here in fear; knowing that you were not redeemed with corruptible things, like silver or gold, from your aimless conduct received by tradition from your fathers, but with the precious blood of Christ, as of a lamb without blemish and without spot. (1 Peter 1:17-19)

We are redeemed from all that is unholy. In this redeemed state, we become the bride of Christ. Our passion then for the bridegroom should both arise out of the holy state into which we are placed and deepen because of our relationship with Christ.

All of the judging (or lack thereof on our parts) is truly God's business. You may choose to hide behind your "judge not" façade, but you cannot escape the command to be holy for that command lines up perfectly with God's purpose and our passion.

A passionate holiness, then, becomes the evidence of a living relationship with Jesus. "Now may the God of peace Himself sanctify you completely; and may your whole spirit, soul, and body be preserved blameless at the coming of our Lord Jesus Christ. He who calls you is faithful, who also will do it. (1 Thessalonians 5:23-24)

How is holiness possible in the lives of sinful men and women? How can we even think that we could pull off being holy as God is holy? Is it even possible to imagine a passionate relationship with Christ that is evidenced by a life of holiness?

The answer to these questions all hinge on the few words found in 1 Thessalonians 5:24. God is expecting to find a blameless and perfect bride at His coming. Even though we are not in a perfect state of holiness now, we are in a process of sanctification through which God is bringing about His holiness in each of our lives. Paul declares that God is working toward this end as he tells us, "He who calls you is faithful, who also will do it."

There is the blessed answer to those hard questions I asked above. How is holiness possible? He is faithful! How can we be as holy as God? He calls us into the process according to His purpose which cannot fail! Is it even possible to be passionately holy? He will do it!

The evidence of our passion is guaranteed by our betrothal to Jesus. Paul told the church at Corinth that he was filled with a zealous desire for their holiness. "For I am jealous for you with godly jealousy. For I have betrothed you to one husband, that I may present you as a chaste virgin to Christ." (2 Corinthians 11:2)

Paul saw himself as a spiritual father to the church. He had arranged the marriage of these believers (the bride) to Jesus (the Bridegroom). Now with a white hot zeal he sought to keep this bride ready for the soon coming of her Bridegroom. He was in a positive way jealous over this church which resulted in a protective mode guarding her holiness until she could be presented to her Groom.

It is with this same jealousy that we should guard our own lives so we might be presented to Christ at His coming as a chaste, pure virgin. Never should it be said that we have hidden behind the lame excuse of "judge not" so we could live our lives as we please. We are now married to Christ. Our holiness is expected as evidence of our passion.

Our Passion is Based on the Gift of Salvation

Perhaps this is where all of my discussion of the evidence of passion in the Christian life should have begun. Without the gift of salvation there simply could never be any passion on our part. You see, we love Him because He first loved us (1 John 4:19). Without God initiating His divine passion towards us, we would have no hope of responding with a passion of our own.

Beginning at the point of salvation might have made more sense, but truthfully, many need to go back well before the moment of salvation to understand the complexity of passion as an evidence for the Christian life. Therefore, I have written about the grace of God at work in us, the guidebook of Scripture as our source of understanding passion, and the fact that passion is a guarantee that holiness will be always preeminent in the Christian life.

That brings us to the moment when salvation takes place. The lost and errant soul comes into the full realization that God passionately loves him or her. In that transaction, we are swept away into His ardent and boundless love and suddenly we realize that we can love Him in return!

Unfortunately, we can get overwhelmed in the reality of such a demonstration of divine passion and forget that we did not start this process. It all began with God, but it is not intended to stop there. Our passion which is derived from this new found relationship prompts us to openly and unashamedly proclaim our connection to the God who saved us by His grace. When the gift of salvation is fully understood, we will be like a new bride who is often said to glow with the radiance of her love for her groom.

The evidence of our passion based on the fact that we have been saved gives us all the reason we need to share the hope that is in us. This sharing of hope in Christ is the very will of God for us. "To them God willed to make known what are the riches of the glory of this mystery among the Gentiles: which is Christ in you, the hope of glory." (Colossians 1:27)

Notice that we do not share out of our own resources. We tell the world about the riches of His glory and the joy of His hope. All of this is contained in the one simple fact: CHRIST IN US! Apart from that truth, we have nothing of which to tell.

The glow of our relationship with Christ is the driving force of our communicating our passion for Him who loved us and gave Himself to us totally. We see this in the prayer that Paul prayed for the Ephesians, "that the God of our Lord Jesus Christ, the Father of glory, may give to you the spirit of wisdom and revelation in the knowledge of Him, the eyes of your understanding being enlightened; that you may know what is *the hope of His calling*, what *are the riches of the glory of His inheritance* in the saints, [19] and what is *the exceeding greatness of His power toward us who believe*, according to the working of His mighty power which He worked in Christ when He raised Him from the dead and seated Him at His right hand in the heavenly places, far above all principality and power and might and dominion, and every name that is named, not only in this age but also in that which is to come. [emphasis mine]" (Ephesians 1:17-21)

Having experienced this deep level of love from none other than God Himself, it becomes clear very quickly that our passion cannot be contained in the privacy of relationship alone. Our passion is after all an evidence of our claim to Christianity. What good is a proof that is never put before the public eye?

The display of our passion is not something that is done in an accidental, haphazard way. We place the evidence of passion before the world with intentional design and under orders of the Bridegroom Himself. The last words of commission by Jesus to his disciples were recorded in Matthew's gospel.

"Go therefore and make disciples of all the nations, baptizing them in the name of the Father and of the Son and of the Holy Spirit, teaching them to observe all things that I have commanded you; and lo, I am with you always, even to the end of the age." (Matthew 28:19-20)

Our passion for Jesus moves us to tell others of His love for us and for them. Our efforts result in others coming to know His passion and knowing for the first time what it means to be loved by the Divine. The wonder of it all is that He has promised to be right there with us when we introduce Him to others. Like a husband or wife introducing their spouse to a stranger, we stand in tandem with the Savior of the world and openly declare our love for Him.

Doing so, declares publicly that we were loved first and opens the door for others to come to know Christ passionately as well. There is an unloved world that will marvel at your passion if you only tell the story of how He first loved you.

Mileposts

List some synonyms that come to mind when you think of the word passion.

_____

_____

_____

_____

How can mere human passion be affected by resources or circumstance?

_____

_____

_____

_____

What are the four ways the author details as demonstrators of passion?

_____

_____

_____

_____

Why can passion never be based on second hand information?

_____

_____

_____

_____

How does the evidence of passion differ from mere emotional response?

_____

_____

_____

_____

In what ways does Scripture help to define love as the basis of true passion?

_____

_____

_____

_____

Describe the element of holiness as it relates to passion's work in the life of a Christian.

_____

_____

_____

_____

The gift of salvation prompts us to openly display our passion in what prominent ways?

_____

_____

_____

_____

NOTES

Chapter Five

THE PROSPERING

When people attempt to evaluate the Christian life sooner or later they come to this question: "What's in it for me?" Somehow we always condense it all down to a matter of personal gain or, if you will, dollars and cents.

The pages of history and the street corners in your town have seen those who have "sold" the gospel come and go. The health and wealth crowd seems to always have a following. Many hear the siren call of name it and claim it or as I like to put it: Blab it and grab it!

Jesus had His crowds as well. Those who were looking for the next miracle. The multitudes who were waiting for the next breaking of the loaves and dividing of the fish. He was very different in His response to the crowds though when compared to this day and time.

Where many today would begin a building fund to accommodate the overflow, Jesus offered for them to eat of

His body and drink His blood. The results: "From that time many of His disciples went back and walked with Him no more." (John 6:66)

There is strong evidence that the crowds who were seeking to prosper in their everyday circumstance did not impress Jesus for He "had no need that anyone should testify of man, for He knew what was in man." (John 2:25)

So, why a chapter on prospering? God really does intend for the Christian personally and for the church corporately to proper. It is the terms of prospering that are very different than the pattern seen over and again in those who would prosper in some physical sense.

Our prospering can take on many forms, but I will only consider three. These three are revealed clearly in Paul's second letter to the church at Thessalonica. As this letter begins, Paul addresses the church and tells them that he offers thanks to God for three evidences of prosperity in their lives.

These three qualities are: faith, love, and patience. Paul uses words like "grows" and "abounds" to describe these marks of prosperity.

Here's how he wrote it as he began his letter: "Paul, Silvanus, and Timothy, to the church of the Thessalonians in God our Father and the Lord Jesus Christ: Grace to you and peace from God our Father and the Lord Jesus Christ. We are bound to thank God always for you, brethren, as it is fitting, because your *faith grows* exceedingly, and the *love of every one of you all abounds* toward each other, so that we ourselves boast of you among the churches of God for your *patience* and faith in all your persecutions and tribulations that you endure," (2 Thessalonians 1:1-4) [*emphasis mine*]

A Prospering Christian Is One Whose Faith Is Growing

Prosperity does not come naturally or easily to the believer no more than a harvest just pops out of the ground for the farmer. There are days of preparation, planting, and persevering until the fruits can be picked and enjoyed by the farmer. So, the Christian will experience the full joy of faith not in the beginning, but in the end.

Paul commends the church at Thessalonica for their faith and the fact that their faith was growing in an amazingly, abundant fashion. To better understand what this word faith means, you need to grasp its full meaning.

The Greek word translated as faith in the preceding verses is *pistis*. It holds the idea of believing or conviction. It is a word that assumes an object. In this case, the faith spoken of is the assuring belief placed upon Christ as Savior.

More than a generic faith, the faith that Paul refers to is particular to salvation. In the original text the article "the" or "this" would be provided. Paul was not speaking of the Thessalonians ability to have faith or to grow their faith through some natural means. He thanked God for *the faith* that was growing in miraculous ways in their lives. This was the faith that could only come as a gift from God at the moment of salvation.

As Paul had written previously to the Ephesian church, "For by grace you have been saved through faith, and that not of yourselves; it is the gift of God, not of works, lest anyone should boast." (Ephesians 2:8-9)

This faith which was found in an overflowing fashion in the lives of the Thessalonians was the gift of God. They could not boast of it for it was not of their own design. And yet, Paul could give thanks back to God for this evidence of a prospering faith in the lives of these believers. Herein is the fruit of this faith harvest: We are the recipients of true faith at work in our lives as evidenced by the fact that it is growing outside of our control or influence.

This does not mean that we are simply repositories for faith to reside in and propagate itself. We have real responsibilities to make sure that faith can grow in us. Like the farmer, the ground must be tilled, weeds pulled, fertilizer applied, regular watering maintained, and a watchful eye placed on the border of our fields, so that no tares are planted by the enemy in the night.

The word faith is used twice in these first four verse of First Thessalonians. As noted, the first instance has in the original text the article attached specifying a particular, one-of-a-kind faith. The second time the word faith is used the article is not included.

Paul told the Thessalonians, "we ourselves boast of you among the churches of God for your patience and faith in all your persecutions and tribulations that you endure…"(1:4) The faith that is functioning here is not salvation faith, but a measure of faith that is granted by God to face certain times of trial and circumstance. So Paul mentions in Romans 12:3, " …God has dealt to each one a measure of faith."

What part then do we play as Christians in developing a life of faith? How can we prosper in our faith as believers? There are three ways that we can be sure that our faith is growing: seeking, feeding, and exercising.

A growing faith must be sought. This may seem like it is counter intuitive to my previous comments about faith.

Especially the fact that faith is the gift of God and that it is not a natural quality in the human life.

That is the very reason that faith must be sought. It comes from an outside source, but it is apparent that it can be obtained for the asking. We learn this from the actions of the disciples. Luke records in his gospel that the disciples asked Jesus to increase their faith (Luke 17:5).

What was the context of this request? This is very important to understanding their seeking after an additional gift of faith in their lives. They used the word increase in their request. This word means to add, give more, proceed further, to place in addition to that already obtained.

Jesus had just finished telling them that offenses would come their way. Not only would troubles come, but they would come multiple times. Sometimes these trials would come time and again in the same day. He told them if a brother offended them seven times in a single day and asked for their forgiveness, they were to forgive him each time.

Their response was, "Increase our faith!"

You have probably been in similar situations where only an infusion of faith would see you through the melee. I am so glad that Luke recorded this instance in the disciples life for us. The disciples were not rebuked by Jesus for their request. His response was one of tenderness as He gave instruction about the power of just a little faith.

"So the Lord said, 'If you have faith as a mustard seed, you can say to this mulberry tree, 'Be pulled up by the roots and be planted in the sea,' and it would obey you.'" (Luke 17:6)

Connected to this illustration of faith's power, Jesus then tells the disciples a story of a man who has servants who have worked all day. When they come into the house they are not at liberty to eat and rest. They must first prepare a meal for the master. Only after he has completed his meal can they then sit down to their supper.

Jesus' conclusion to this parable is that in all of this the servant is not profitable. He has only performed the minimum requirement for which he was hired.

This is the lesson of faith. We have not been saved to be static. Our faith should never be dwarfed, but dynamic and growing to its full potential. This is why Paul thanked God for the exceptional growth of the faith found in the Thessalonians. Faith, as found among these believers, was extraordinary!

Would you join the disciples today in whatever circumstance you find yourself? Ask God to increase your faith to the point that someone might pray like Paul did and thank God for your faith life.

A faith like this is not a once and done deal. It is a vibrant living process and like all living things it must be fed regularly. How can our faith be fed so the growth never ends?

Faith feeds upon the word of God. Not only does it feed upon the word, it literally comes into existence by the word of God. Paul told the Romans, "So then faith comes by hearing, and hearing by the word of God." Faith leaps into being when the word of God is heard.

This is not passive in nature, but active. When a person purposefully listens to God's word then faith leaps into motion and begins to grow as it is fed by the word.

I am not speaking here of the mere reading or listening to the reading of some Bible passage. If faith came by simple exposure to the words of the Bible, then we would do well to post them everywhere. We could do one better than the Gideons by not only placing a Bible in the nightstand by the bed of each motel room, but by writing Bible passages on the nightstand itself!

Now certainly all of those Bibles placed around the world by Gideons have proven to be an excellent tool of evangelism. None of those who came to know the saving faith of God were saved, however, by merely opening a Bible and reading the printed words.

It was only when those printed words became in that moment the *very words of God*, that salvation took place. That is what happens as described by Paul in Romans 10:17.

He uses a particular Greek word which is translated as *word* in the English language. Paul chose the word *rhema* for use in this verse. *Rhema* can be defined as a particular thought or command for a very specific person, purpose, or period.

Faith then come into existence when the word (*logos*) of God becomes the *rhema* of God. In that instant a person hears what God is saying directly to them and by that word comes to know the faith of God at work in their lives.

Just as the word of God plays a vital part in the birth of faith, so the word of God is integral to the growth of faith. The writer of Hebrews describes a person who is a believer, but they are not thriving. "For though by this time you ought to be teachers, you need someone to teach you again the first principles of the oracles of God; and you have come to need milk and not solid food. For everyone who partakes only of milk is unskilled in the word of righteousness, for he is a babe. But solid food belongs to those who are of full age, that is, those who by reason of use have their senses exercised to discern both good and evil." (Hebrews 5:12-14)

The faith life described here is not maturing as it should because these believers are not consuming the meat of the word. They are only ingesting milk like a newborn. Conversely, those who are growing are filled with solid food (the word of God) and are exercising their faith so it can be strengthened.

That brings us to the third part of assuring a growing faith. We must exercise the faith we have. It's the old "use it or lose it" rule. Any increase in faith we may obtain by asking and seeking will soon wither if it is not utilized regularly in the Christian's life.

A.W. Tozer is quoted in *The Best of A.W. Tozer Book Two* as saying, "Faith enables our spiritual sense to function. Where faith is defective the result will be inward insensibility and numbness toward spiritual things. This is the condition of vast numbers of Christians today."

We have become fat and lazy Christians who just cannot bring ourselves to get off the spiritual couch or may I say the pew! We sit and complain about our poverty or point accusing fingers at those who seem to be prospering in the faith. All the while we explain away the answer to our condition. We assume that prosperity in the Christian life only means money in the bank.

We sit and watch some television religious personality tell us to just name it and claim—blab it and grab it. But honestly, we don't have enough faith to do either, even if it came by such low means.

Several years ago Amy Grant sang a song written by Steve Millikan and Rodney Robison. The song is entitled, "Fat Baby". The lyrics are expressive when it comes to describing the Christian whose faith has not been fed nor has it been exercised.

> I know a man maybe you know him, too
> You never can tell he might even be you
> He knelt at the altar and that was the end
> He's saved and that's all that matters to him
>
> His spiritual tummy it can't take too much
> One day a week he gets his spiritual lunch
> On Sunday he puts on his spiritual best
> And gives his language a spiritual rest
>
> He's been baptized, sanctified redeemed by the blood
> But his daily devotions are stuck in the mud
> He knows the books of the Bible and John 3:16
> He's got the biggest King James you've ever seen
>
> I've always wondered if he'll grow up someday
> He's momma's boy and he likes it that way
> If you happen to see him tell him I said
> He'll never grow if he never gets fed
>
> He's just a fat little baby
> He wants his bottle and he don't mean maybe
> He's sampled solid food once or twice
> But he says doctrine leaves him cold as ice
>
> He's just a fat, fat, fat, fat, fat, fat, fat
> A fat, fat, fat, fat, fat, fat, fat
> A fat, fat, fat, fat, fat, fat, fat, little baby

This song really tells the whole story of what happens when a Christian does not prosper by growing in the faith. As James clearly states in his epistle, "Thus also faith by itself, if it does not have works, is dead." (James 2:17)

We can never work to gain faith, but when faith is claimed and no works follow then it is easily dismissed as non-biblical faith. As we work out the Christian life our faith is energized, strengthened, and prospers. (Philippians 2:12-13)

A Prospering Christian Is One Whose Love Is Growing

There is probably no word that is more thrown about in a haphazard way in this day than the word love. Love is attached to so many things that it has become meaningless to most people.

We love everything from hamburgers to houses, pets to people, and cars to cruises. Love seems to apply to any item which has fallen into our purview of delight. It does, however, prove that love demands an object even when the use of the word is misplaced.

Love like faith cannot exist alone. Faith requires works to validate it. Love requires an object upon which it might display its essence. Try to have faith in faith or speak the word love without giving it an object and the concepts are meaningless.

Paul declares that the Thessalonians were not only growing in their faith, but their love was abounding. He uses the word *agape* to identify the love of the Thessalonians as more than some emotional frenzy. Their love was of a godly nature. It was a love that was based upon the very character of God and impossible to exhibit apart from being a Christian.

Love is clearly the greatest attribute of all and is a primary evidence of Christianity itself. Paul in writing to the church at Corinth said of love, "And now abide faith, hope, love, these three; but the greatest of these is love." (1 Corinthians 13:13) Faith is listed, as well as hope, which we will speak of later in the essence of patience. But greater than either faith or hope is love.

Scripture is ripe with references to the subject of love. Jesus declared that love would be the identifier of His disciples (John 13:35). He declared that a man could have no greater love than to lay down his life for a friend (John 15:13). Paul wrote the entirety of First Corinthians 13 about love. John filled his first epistle with multiple references relating to love. Therein, he declares that a person cannot know God or be a Christian while not loving his brother (1 John 3:10). These are but a few of the places throughout scripture that speak of the primary importance of love.

We cannot throw aside any of the other evidences of Christianity for this one attribute, however. As a matter of fact, I believe that Paul listed the three qualities of a prospering church in the order which he did for a specific reason. If love is primary, why not name it first?

Faith is mentioned first, because faith puts us in contact with the God who is love and through Him alone can we ever have the ability to love in a Christ-like fashion. Not only will we be able to love, but this love will abound in the same degree that love abounds in God Himself. In John's first epistle as mentioned above, God is defined by love. Love is not only an attribute of God, but it is part of His very essence. John says twice in First John 4:8 and 4:16, "God is love." Until a person believes and abides in the love of God, that person is not a Christian.

Here is why faith precedes love in Paul's letter. Salvation comes by faith (Galatians 2:8) and until a person is brought to life through the work of God's grace they can never know God's love. We love because He first loved us (1 John 4:19).

Paul used the adjective abound to describe the love of the Thessalonians. The Greek word from which abound is translated is where we get the English word "plenty." The idea is that of a super-abounding love that exists in abundance that is ever increasing unto the point of always being plentiful. They were loving in such a way that no person or situation would be addressed without the element of love being integral to the equation.

This plenteous love reminds me of the response that was always given in the home in which I was reared. It never mattered who dropped by at supper time. They were invited to sit at our table and partake of the meal. Somehow the food that had been prepared was always enough. It was of an ever-increasing quality that met the needs of our guests.

This kind of love is the symbol of maturity in the life of a Christian and in the life of the church. Paul wrote to the Colossians on this very subject and noted, "But above all these things put on love, which is the bond of perfection." (Colossians 3:14) Perfection here is not a state of sinlessness. It is to reach full growth, become of age, to be complete. Just as we never stop growing until we die, so our love should always be abounding unto a point of maturity that cannot be moved by circumstance or quandary. We can join the Thessalonians in facing every trial and tribulation with an overflowing abundance of love.

Life will always throw us a curve or two when we least expect it. Questions will arise that seem to have no answers and if we are not careful we will leave the critical standard of love out of our search for the truth.

Once again scripture, which speaks so often of love, gives us the answer to what can seem like a dilemma. Paul declares to the church at Ephesus that love is the key to understanding such impossible moments along our journey.

Paul is once again in prayer mode in the third chapter of his epistle to the Ephesians. He says, "…that Christ may dwell in your hearts through faith; that you, being rooted and grounded in love, may be able to comprehend with all the saints what is the width and length and depth and height—to know the love of Christ which passes knowledge; that you may be filled with all the fullness of God. …" (Ephesians 1:17-19)

Do you see the same ordering of faith and love once again as Paul prays for the Ephesians? He clearly states that Christ only dwells in the human heart as a work of faith. But closely following this thought is the fact that our confidence as a Christian (an evidence, if you please) will be rooted and grounded in love. Love then provides for us as Christians a stable foundation upon which we can build our claim to a relationship in Christ Jesus.

But here is the bonus! With this foundation of love securely fixed, we have understanding of the love of Christ which surpasses our ability to know. Now that's a thought which is not easily comprehended!

When love is at its full level of maturity, providing a stable foundation for the Christian life, we are, then and only then, able to fully grasp the overwhelming dimensions of the love God has for us.

Again, we love Him, because He first loved us (1 John 4:19).

A Prospering Christian Is One Whose Patience Is Growing

The final element that we will discuss in this journey towards prosperity is patience. I have not saved the best for last. I am simply following Paul's format. It is, however, best that we are considering patience last since it is often the most difficult for us to obtain or live out on a daily basis.

I am grateful that you have had the *patience* to get this far along in this Bible study!

Now patience is not natural and in this day and time it is in short supply. That in itself is an oxymoron since patience should never run short. Yet it does for all of us most of the time.

We avoid the subject. We certainly don't want to be reminded of everyone's favorite Bible verse on patience, "And not only so, but we glory in tribulations also: knowing that tribulation works patience…" (Romans 5:3) Who in their right mind would ask for patience after discovering that it only comes by way of tribulation? Yet Paul commends the Thessalonians for their patience to the point of boasting about it.

He plainly and unashamedly declares, "...that we ourselves boast of you among the churches of God for your patience and faith in all your persecutions and tribulations that you endure..." (2 Thessalonians 1:4)

Even in this verse patience is directly connected to persecutions and tribulations. It seems to be made clear that patience comes only in the face of the trial. Without the testing patience has no basis for existing.

So then, patience is connected in an intricate way to both the matters of faith and love that have been previously discussed. In both cases, faith and love demand an object. Patience needs not an object, but a catalyst. It simply will not be found without the prompting of tribulation.

The word *patience* means a steadfast endurance. It is more than just putting up with something until it passes or ends. This response to difficulty begins early and ends late. In reality it never ends. If it did have an end then it could not be defined as enduring.

The original language attaches a definite article to the word which helps us understand that this is no generic patience. It is *the* patience as in a particular kind of patience that can only be found rarely. It is so rare that it is boasted of when found. So, Paul brags about *the patience* of the Thessalonians in the face of such persecution and tribulation. He even includes the ending phrase, that you endure, so we can know that this is no ordinary form of patience.

Incredibly, this kind of patience has attached to it a cheerfulness and hopefulness that goes beyond the natural response or instinct of mortality. It is one thing to wait patiently; it is quite another to do so with joy.

This patient response found in the Thessalonian church is an indication that they were prospering. The patience demonstrated in their lives as believers was not static, but dynamic. It was growing as the threats increased.

Three truths can be discovered in the light of patience that is growing in the life of a Christian. A growing patience allows us to accomplish God's will, allows us to achieve satisfaction in life, and allows us to be ready for the appearance of Christ in His second coming.

Hang a sign in a window that a class will assemble around the topic of knowing God's will and you may not have enough room for the students. Everyone is interested in knowing God's will for their lives. Amazingly, the Bible gives us a real sneak peek into the matter, but you may not like what you will see.

Hebrews 10:26 tells us that patience is directly linked to accomplishing God's will. "For you have need of patience, that, after ye have done the will of God, ye might receive the promise." Patience is the prerequisite to doing the will of God and to receiving the promises of God in our lives.

It just may be that God's will for you is to simply endure what you are going through at this very moment. So often we want God's will to change our situation, but in the case of the Thessalonians, God's will was to endure the persecution! And remember, this is not just muttering through your circumstances. That little element of joy should be present in the equation. Only then will we grow in patience and thereby fulfill the will of God.

By the way, the promise follows in Hebrews 10:38: "Now the just shall live by faith..." That's going to take some more patience!

As your patience increases you will become more and more satisfied with your position in life. You may have noticed that everyone doesn't get to be rich; everyone will not graduate from college; everyone will not grow up to be a doctor or lawyer. Even though we know these facts to be true, there is still that insatiable desire for more. It always seems that the Joneses are winning in the challenge to have more or be more and we are more than willing to keep up our part in the challenge.

The Apostle Paul said that he had learned to be content in every state in which he found himself (Philippians 4:11). The ability to do this was not found in himself but in Christ who strengthened him (Philippians 4:13). By using the word strengthened here, Paul directs us back to the idea of an increasing process. In verse 12 of this same chapter he says, "I know how to be abased, and I know how to abound. Everywhere and in all things I have learned both to be full and to be hungry, both to abound and to suffer need." (Philippians 4:12)

It is the mystery of suffering and need that teaches us patience and thereby brings us to the place of contentment and satisfaction. James instructs us on this same principle of patience and the subsequent satisfaction that comes when patience is allowed to accomplish its ultimate goal: "But let patience have its perfect work, that you may be perfect and complete, lacking nothing." (James 1:4)

Imagine for a moment how you feel after you have consumed a huge delicious meal. All courses were well prepared, seasoned perfectly, and served at just the right temperature. You push away from the table and proclaim with a deep sigh, "I cannot eat another bite!" You are completely satisfied as far as your hunger is concerned.

This is the very picture of patience having made you perfect and complete. You are fully mature and whole in every part of your life as a result of patience running its course. You can know that you are growing as a believer when you sense that fullness of body, mind, and soul that comes no matter the circumstance. You are in the same state as the Apostle Paul declared himself: **content!**

Now before you line up to eat your fill at the table of contentment, realize that none of this happens overnight. Remember, this all happens as patience has her will and way in your life. A.T. Robertson said in *Word Pictures In the New Testament*, "Mushrooms spring up overnight, but they are usually poisonous. The best fruits require time, cultivation, patience." His remarks were in reference to the parable of the sower and the seed that fell on good ground. Again, patience is demanded if the satisfaction of a good harvest is to be reaped.

Isobel Kuhn, in *Green Leaf in Drought Time*, said of suffering, "God does not waste suffering.... If he plows it is because he purposes a crop." I remember hearing Rick Warren say, "God never waste suffering. Mushrooms grow overnight, but oaks take a lifetime of storms to mature." Like it or not, patience doesn't come instantaneously.

May I be honest here? I don't like it and neither do you! But anything short of continuance and endurance is simply not patience. We must constantly be guarding our patience and growing ever more patient as our lives unfold.

Here's a good place to ask the age-old question. "Are we there yet?" Well, I'm glad you asked, because I have an answer for you! "We will get there when we get there!"

Now you know why you must be patient. Neither you or I are there yet. But there is good news! There is a sure end to this process of patience. It is the moment that the Lord Himself comes back for us. James said, "Therefore be patient, brethren, until the coming of the Lord. See how the farmer waits for the precious fruit of the earth, waiting patiently for it until it receives the early and latter rain. You also be patient. Establish your hearts, for the coming of the Lord is at hand. (James 5:7-8)

The prospering church is then one whose faith, love, and patience is growing. These three elements are tightly bound together and cannot function long apart from one another. Each one of these characteristics is being developed in you as God brings you through times of suffering, trials, and joy.

At the coming of Jesus, all unfinished work will be completed in an instant as we are changed in a moment, in the twinkling of an eye (1 Corinthians 15:52). When we see Him we will recognize Him in all of His completeness for we shall be as He is—perfect!

"Behold what manner of love the Father has bestowed on us, that we should be called children of God! Therefore the world does not know us, because it did not know Him. 2 Beloved, now we are children of God; and it has not yet been revealed what we shall be, but we know that when He is revealed, we shall be like Him, for we shall see Him as He is. 3 And everyone who has this hope in Him purifies himself, just as He is pure." (1 John 3:1-3)

Mileposts

In what three ways is the prosperity of the believer revealed?

_____

_____

_____

_____

What are three ways that we can be sure that our faith is growing?

_____

_____

_____

_____

How can the growth of our faith be inhibited?

_____

_____

_____

_____

How are faith and love interlinked in our lives?

_____

_____

_____

_____

Why does faith always precede love in Paul's letters?

_____

_____

_____

_____

Why is patience so difficult to master in our lives?

_____

_____

_____

_____

What has God been using in your life to prompt a growing patience?

_____

_____

_____

_____

How does an attitude of contentment lead to deeper level of patience in our lives?

_____

_____

_____

_____

NOTES

Chapter Six

THE PERSEVERANCE

Skeptical!

Perhaps you are like me (maybe I'm seeking sympathy from those of like mind) when it comes to new-fangled ideas or upon hearing that a person has made some radical change in their life. Skepticism seems to be a natural reaction for many. You've probably said something along these lines: "We'll see how long this lasts!"

Healthy skepticism is not bad. It helps us to keep our guards up and ready for that which is deceitful or harmful. Especially in this world of knock-offs it's probably good to kick the proverbial tires and take a bit of a wait and see attitude.

Is there room for skepticism when it comes to a person's claim to Christianity? Should we be "kicking the tires" of those who claim the name of Christ? Is it okay to expect some degree of perseverance from those who call themselves

Christians? Scripture seems to say so. John wrote in his first epistle, "Beloved, do not believe every spirit, but test the spirits, whether they are of God; because many false prophets have gone out into the world." (1 John 4:1) John writes once more in this same letter about the evidence of perseverance, "They went out from us, but they were not of us; for if they had been of us, they would have continued with us; but they went out that they might be made manifest, that none of them were of us." (1 John 2:19)

Throughout scripture we find those who claimed a relationship with God, but later departed from it and thereby proved that there had never been one in the beginning. Unfortunately, this is all too common among people today. This leads one to easily become a bit skeptical when a person declares themselves to be a Christian.

Is there then some evidence of perseverance that we can expect to exist in the life of a believer? Will there be this same perseverance in the church as the common body of all believers? The answer is yes! And the same Bible that speaks of those who departed from the faith is the book which tells us how to persevere.

Paul was a master at describing the Christian life in everyday terminology. He could paint pictures with his words that gave his readers a clear and vivid description. When it comes to the concept of perseverance, Paul used a very common occurrence in the culture of his day. He related the principle of perseverance to effectively running a race.

Sports were as much a part of the lives of first century Christians as they are of our generation. Paul used the two primary events of the Isthmian games to speak to the church at Corinth about the evidence of perseverance in the Christian life.

He said, "Do you not know that those who run in a race all run, but one receives the prize? Run in such a way that you may obtain it. And everyone who competes for the prize is temperate in all things. Now they do it to obtain a perishable crown, but we for an imperishable crown. Therefore I run thus: not with uncertainty. Thus I fight: not as one who beats the air. But I discipline my body and bring it into subjection, lest, when I have preached to others, I myself should become disqualified." (1 Corinthians 9:24-27)

The two events that Paul uses as illustrations are the foot race and boxing. I will use his words to the Corinthians in this chapter on the evidence of perseverance. In a world that is growing more skeptical by the day of Christians and Christianity, there is no greater proof needed that that which can be found in the persevering believer.

Even the portion of the text which speaks of fighting is applicable to the art of running the race. The key to all of this is discipline. Discipline is needed lest the believer is labeled as disqualified and thereby leaves room for the "I told you so!" of the doubting world.

There are three main parts to running the race. A race will not be won unless there is control, confidence, and a conclusion. All of these elements must exist in the running of the race. All of these elements must be found in the believer who will prove his relationship with Christ by running the race of life with perseverance.

The Race Must Be Run With Control

The context of the sporting events of Paul's day and those upon which he drew his illustration were the Isthmian games. These were the precursor of our modern day Olympic games. These games did not include an invitation for the world to participate. The only athletes who could take part in the games were Greeks. Unless you had Grecian citizenship you were prohibited from the events. Similarly, Paul was only speaking to those who held heavenly citizenship.

Certainly an unbeliever can be a committed and disciplined person. Such a person might attain many accolades and accomplish great tasks, but the Christian race can only be run by the born-again believer. This fact proves more often than not who is really a Christian. The stamina and fortitude needed to finish the Christian course is only made possible by the indwelling Christ.

Amazingly, the games Paul referred to had a much different outcome that what we are familiar with in the Olympics. The games of Paul's day had only one winner. Second and third placed were of no consequence. All ran to win knowing that only one could win in the end.

These athletes competed for a simple crown made of perishable material. No gold, silver, or bronze was awarded to the victor. He ran for the emperor and for the glory of Greece. He knew that a laurel wreath upon his brow would be his only prize.

Incredibly, hundreds prepared for these races. They endured great stress and all knew that the rules of the games were stringent. The rules not only governed the race, but also the training. Violation in either case would lead to disqualification.

Consider for how much more we run the Christian race. We run not to obtain a perishable crown, but an imperishable one. A crown that will last beyond this life. A crown that we will gladly lay at the feet of the One who gave His life for us as believers.

This is why our race cannot be run with mere rules. We run knowing that we do not have the ability within ourselves to win. We run with a full sense that the power to do so comes from without, yet dwells within us. We run under the control of the Holy Spirit.

I have never been a runner, but I know that running a race to win has a lot to do with one's focus. The athlete must get into a zone that locks all distractions out of his mind. His concern is only the next step in his lane. There is a goal to finish first, but that goal is only attained if you take each step along the way with abandon.

Vance Havner wrote in *The Vance Havner Devotinal Treasury* about the exhortation of R.A. Torrey. Dr. Torrey had said to him while he was still a young preacher, "Young man, make up your mind on one thing and stick to it." Havner comments on this thought, "The Christian life should be like a sword with one point, not like a broom ending in many straws. Such a single purpose forgets the past, reaches toward the future, and presses on. There is no time or place for side issues, diversions to the right or to the left. There is no place for hands on the plow with eyes looking back."

This aptly describes the focus that is necessary to run the race with the intent of winning. The athlete may ask, "Can't I smoke, drink, and have a good time while I train for the race?" The coach will respond, "Yes, you can. But you cannot win!" Athletes must understand that discipline means giving up the good and even the better so they can obtain the best. This should be the ideal of the Christian believer as the race is run to completion.

I have heard many descriptions of the race we run as Christians. Of course, the runners of Paul's day would have trained for the marathon. Endurance would have been the key to winning such a race. In some ways, we too are running a marathon. Each of us engaged in our individual race to the finish line as noted in Hebrews 12:1, "Therefore we also, since we are surrounded by so great a cloud of witnesses, let us lay aside every weight, and the sin which so easily ensnares us, and let us run with endurance the race that is set before us..."

Some have used the dash to describe our running of the race. We have only a brief time to complete the challenge and then the race is done. In some ways this description is like the birth and death dates on a tombstone. The dates mark the beginning and the ending. The dash that separates these dates is where we live. The words of Moses as recorded in Psalm 90 tells us the story of the dash. "The days of our lives are seventy years; and if by reason of strength they are eighty years, — So teach us to number our days, that we may gain a heart of wisdom." (Psalm 90:10a, 12)

I do not see the full story of our race in the dash. Nor would I use the sprint to explain our running. Sprinting has its purpose for surely there are times that we must pour all we have into the race of life. Sprinters, however, will soon fade. The training of the sprinter is to equip for sudden and short burst of energy. The Christian life needs something for the long haul.

It is the relay race that most correctly fits the model of running necessary for the Christian. The relay race encompasses the qualities of all types of races. It has a goal in focus like a marathon runner. It is a dash for at least one segment of the race. It needs runners who can add the burst of energy found in the sprinter's legs also. There is one distinction that sets the relay race apart from the others: partnership.

Partnership is required as a team of runners work together to complete the task. There must be at some point in the race a moment that the responsibility for running is passed to another runner. Your segment of the race is done and all hopes are placed on the next runner.

The relay race is a beautiful picture of one generation handing to the next the challenge of finishing the race set before them. My generation and yours must run with diligence, but we must be ready for the moment of transition to the one who runs the next segment of the race.

The relay runner is the only runner that carries an object through the race. All other racers are free of responsibility to the other runners. Not so with the relay runner. Each person in this style of racing must carefully handle and pass on to the next runner the baton.

The modern baton is about 12 inches long and weighs a mere 1.76 ounces. It is designed in such a way that it will not be a burden to the runner and allow for an effortless transfer to the next runner. The baton reminds me of the words of Jesus in Matthew's gospel. "Come to Me, all you who labor and are heavy laden, and I will give you rest. Take My yoke upon you and learn from Me, for I am gentle and lowly in heart, and you will find rest for your souls. For My yoke is easy and My burden is light." (Matthew 11:28-30)

In the midst of our labor we are promised rest. This rest does not relinquish us of our responsibilities, however. The promise of Jesus is that He will replace our heavy burden with one that is light—one as light as a baton used in the relay race of life.

There is a danger here. The risk is revealed in the very nature of a burden that is so light we forget we are carrying it or we fail to properly transfer this responsibility to the next generation. If we fail in this transition, the team of runners lose the race no matter how fast you may have run.

In the 2008 Beijing Olympics both the men's and women's 4X100 relay was lost because of a dropped baton. Tyson Gay said after the race, "I'm a veteran. I've run all kinds of relays. I've never dropped a baton in my life. It's kind of upsetting. I can't believe it." This was the first time the United States failed to medal in this race. The athletes had not failed to train. Their bodies were of elite status. The track was of highest quality. There was no defect in the baton. Each team simply dropped a 1.76 ounce piece of aluminum and lost the race. Unbelievable, but true.

The race we run is ours, but we have another leg (generation) ahead of us. They are counting on us to handle the responsibilities of our segment and always be ready to hand off the baton to them. All of this takes control.

Shortly after Paul "Bear" Bryant, the famed college football coach, died his family found a piece of crumpled, yellowed paper in his wallet. From its condition it appeared that he had carried it for years. The folds in the paper had been worn thin from folding and unfolding many times. The following words were written on this piece of paper: "This is the beginning of a new day. God has given me this day to use as I will; I can waste it, or use it for good. What I do today is very important because I am exchanging a day of my life for it. When tomorrow comes this day will be gone forever leaving something in its place that I've traded for it. I want it to be a gain, not a loss; good, not evil; success, not failure, in order that I shall not regret the price I paid for it."

Let it never be said of your race, "I can't believe that I dropped the baton!" Finish well!

The Race Must Be Run with Confidence

The positive side of perseverance is finishing the race and receiving the prize. In this case, a mere laurel wreath is all the glory the winner could expect in tangible terms. The greater satisfaction was found in the honor bestowed by the king or other magistrate that would award the simple wreath.

The negative side of the persevering race cannot be ignored. Paul addresses this as he closes out his discourse on running the race with perseverance. He uses strong wording that includes in verses 26 and 27 these phrases:

> not with uncertainty
> not as one who beats the air
> lest … I become disqualified.

Paul said that he ran his race "not with uncertainty." The idea here is that he ran with full disclosure and determination. His path was clearly delineated. He knew where he was headed and refused to be taken off course. The same word translated as uncertainty in verse 26 is used by Jesus as he described the hidden condition of the scribes and Pharisees.

The scribes and Pharisees lived their lives in such a way that they were not only a danger to themselves, but posed a direct danger to others. Luke records the words of Jesus as he calls these men hypocrites and pronounces their lives to be like undisclosed graves which posed great danger to travelers. "Woe to you, scribes and Pharisees, hypocrites! For you are like graves which are not seen, and the men who walk over them are not aware of them." (Luke 11:44)

Others who followed these men risked the danger of their uncertain teaching and the result would be like falling into an unmarked open grave. Paul knew that the race was his alone to run, but others would follow the path he left behind. He wanted to run with such confidence that he could finish well and help others who would follow him to do the same.

How could he have such a high level of confidence? Was it his education? His upbringing? How about his heritage?

None of these external qualities could help him run this race to the finish and do so in such a way as to encourage us who run today to do the same. The power to run like this comes from an internal source that is not natural to mankind. It is the indwelling presence of the Holy Spirit that keeps us on track and gives us the certainty to run until the race is done.

There will always be distractions as we run, but you must determine that these sideshows will not pull you off course. There will always be disappointments that will make every attempt to drain you of your hope and vision of the finish line. We must form the resolve of the Scottish theologian Samuel Rutherford. He said, "Believe in God's love and power more than you believe in your own feelings and experiences. Your rock is Christ, and it is not the rock that ebbs and flows, but your sea of feelings."

At this point Paul mixes his metaphors and includes the sport of boxing in his racing illustration. He does not do so haphazardly, however. The boxing or fighting metaphor serves well as he transitions to the discipline required to finish the race.

Paul declares that his fighting is real. It is not some imaginary foe that he is matched up against in the ring of life nor is he simply shadow boxing.

It is from this analogy that he speaks of the personal discipline that controls his life. It is as if he steps apart from himself and speaks of the discipline that he subjects himself to as a regular routine in his life; training, if you will, in such a way that he can obtain the prize.

The literal meaning of discipline is to hit under the eye, i.e., to give a black eye. In Paul's case his fighting is not against some unnamed shadowy character. His opponent is himself and his discipline is at such a heightened level that in essence he gives himself a black eye.

When you see a person with a blackened eye, you know immediately that there has been an encounter of some sort. Some black eyes may come accidentally, but not so with Paul. He disciplined his body into subjection and like a "shiner" on his face discipline was evident as having occurred.

The confidence it takes to run the race of life well and run it to the conclusion will never be found in an undisciplined life. Some want to run the race like joggers in the park. For the most part many part-time runners do so with little attention paid to the process of running. You will see these people with earbuds crammed in their ears as they listen to a myriad of sounds disassociated from the race at hand. They may be pushing a baby stroller or handling a dog on a leash, but their running is secondary.

The disciplined runner is a disciple of the process. Look closely at the word discipline and you will see at its root the word disciple. In one sense disciple is the *root* of discipline and discipline if the *route* of the disciple. You simply cannot have one without the other. Unlike the weekend jogger, the real runner will always be about the process of running. All attention will be directed to the next step and ultimately to crossing the finish line *in first place!*

George Washington said of discipline: "Discipline is the soul of an army. It makes small numbers formidable, procures success to the weak and esteem to all [who are governed thereby.]" So it is with each of us as we are called to follow in the example given to us by the Apostle Paul. Neither size or ability makes any difference. Experience is not part of the equation used to bring about discipline. It is the willingness to give yourself a black eye as evidence of the confidence obtained through a life of discipline.

Spiritual discipline then is developed by bodily restraint and bodily response. It may begin with a "black eye", but it always results in a deeper and more committed walk with Christ. Billy Graham stated it succinctly when he said, "We believe to become a Christian, we behave because we are."

If it was merely restraint, then the law would have provided all we needed to be disciples. The law needed a bodily response to its demands to be successful and that's where the failure occurs—not in the law, for it is perfect: "The law of the Lord is perfect, converting the soul; the testimony of the Lord is sure, making wise the simple;" (Psalm 19:7) —but in us, for we cannot keep the law in any way: "For we know that the law is spiritual, but I am carnal, sold under sin. For what I am doing, I do not understand. For what I will to do, that I do not practice; but what I hate, that I do. If, then, I do what I will not to do, I agree with the law that it is good." (Romans 7:14-16)

We are limited then in our discipline by the unwillingness to bring our bodies into subjection. Oswald Chambers spoke of this connection between the body and spirit. He noted that "our spirit goes no further than we bring our body." It is simply impossible to live as a disconnected disciple.

Samson is a prime example of this.

Samson sought to live a life dedicated as a Nazarite, yet be fully engaged in the world. He wanted the strength of the Lord upon his life, but did not wish to live under the discipline required and needed to maintain this vital connection. In the end, his failure came when he knew not the Spirit of the Lord had departed from him (Judges 16:20). He fell captive to the Philistines and spent the remainder of his life under their control even though God briefly restored unto him his strength as he destroyed the Philistines in their temple. An undisciplined life took his life at the end.

Paul set no time constraints on the subject of discipline. There were no limits as to duration or costs. The implication is that discipline is to be a lifelong characteristic of the believer.

General Charles G. Gordon was an outstanding man of God. His disciplined life was evident in this account of his life.

> *When the English government wanted to reward him for his distinguished service in China, he declined all money and titles. Finally, after much arguing, he accepted a gold medal inscribed with his name and a record of his accomplishments. Following his death, however, it could not be found among his belongings. It was learned that on a certain date he had sent it to Manchester during a famine with the request that it be melted and used to buy bread for the poor. In his private diary for that day were written these words: "The only thing I have, that I value, I have now given to the Lord Jesus."*
> (Encyclopedia of Illustrations #11446).

Gordon's actions were clearly a "shiner" in his life. May it be that all believers run (and fight) in such a way that in the end all that we have has been brought into subjection to Christ alone.

The Race Must Be Run Until The Conclusion

Earlier I wrote of the consequences of running a distracted race. As I draw this section to a close, let me direct your attention towards the finish line. We must run our race for the entire distance. This can only be accomplished with a solid determination.

How can you keep your focus on the finish line when no one knows when the race will ultimately be concluded? The answer is found in understanding exactly what the finish line is and who is eligible to run this race.

The finish line is heaven. It will only be when we have stepped across the line from life to death that we will be able to say that we have finished our race. Here, however, is a bit of danger. It is very easy to begin believing that you are running the race to obtain heaven. This is far from the truth.

We do not run to obtain heaven—we run because we are on our way to heaven. Heaven is already ours. It is promised that we will dwell with Jesus. The race does not prove us worthy of the finish line. The race establishes the fact that we have a right to be on the track. You will finish your race. That's a fact that is indisputable. Jesus is the promised author and finisher of your faith (Hebrews 12:2).

Remember that Paul's example of the race were based upon the Isthmian games. Only Greek citizens could participate in these events. No one ran in the Isthmian games to become a Greek; you ran because you already were Greek.

This is exactly our status as we run the race before us. We are not running to become a believer; we run because we already are believing in Christ and accepting the fact that we will finish our race and be with Him forever!

So why did Paul talk so much about discipline? If we will finish no matter what, then who cares about being faithful unto the end? The danger is not in a lack of completion, but in becoming a castaway along the way.

This is the warning that Paul places upon himself and the warning that is ours today. "But I discipline my body and bring it into subjection, lest, when I have preached to others, I myself should become disqualified." (1 Corinthians 9:27)

The danger lies not in missing the finish line, but in becoming disqualified along the way. Paul uses a very strong word here: *adokimos*. It is translated many ways and each is an attempt to catch some of the idea behind this word.

The root of this word means to be accepted and approved. All of this is negated by the addition of the letter "*a*" to the word. To be *adokimos* is to be found unacceptable, unapproved, or a phony. The consequence is to be castaway or set aside. Yes, you will be carried across the finish line by God's grace, but your race will not have brought glory to God.

Well, you might conclude that getting across the finish line is all that really matters, but I beg to differ. Paul said that he practiced discipline because it is easy to drift off course in such minute ways that it could be too late when you discover the error. The verse above uses the little word, lest, to transition from disciple to disqualification. This little word opens up any and all possibilities of failure. It could have been translated: *if by any means*.

Paul was so conscious of the fact that a great danger exists to all who run the race. A danger that can be found presenting itself in a myriad of ways. All of which produce a disaster. This disaster is two-fold.

First, the runner is disqualified or set aside. That is in and of itself a tragedy. But of greater note, is the fact that Paul was aware of what might happen to all those who had heard him preach. You see, there is so much more to this race than merely crossing the finish line and arriving safely upon the shore of heaven.

Second, we are being watched by others. Some are mere spectators. They encompass the lost world. Those who are watching, but not yet understanding why we are running and to where we are racing. When we drift off course, the lost are affected by our failure.

Others are our fellow runners. When we fail to run our race properly, we affect others who are in the race as well. The writer of Hebrews stated it like this: "Therefore we must give the more earnest heed to the things we have heard, lest we drift away. For if the word spoken through angels proved steadfast, and every transgression and disobedience received a just reward, how shall we escape if we neglect so great a salvation, which at the first began to be spoken by the Lord, and was confirmed to us by those who heard Him..." (Hebrews 2:1-3)

When we fail to run the race to the conclusion with discipline, the results can be catastrophic. We are placed on the shelf and at the same time become a stumbling block to others.

The source of this story is unknown, but it serves as a clear illustration of the importance of both running and finishing the race: A lighthouse along a bleak coast was tended by a keeper who was given enough oil for one month and told to keep the light burning every night. One day a woman asked for oil so that her children could stay warm. Then a farmer came. His son needed oil for a lamp so he could read. Still another needed some for an engine. The keeper saw each as a worthy request and measured out just enough oil to satisfy all. Near the end of the month, the tank in the lighthouse ran dry. That night the beacon was dark and three ships crashed on the rocks. More than 100 lives were lost.

When a government official investigated, the man explained what he had done and why. "You were given one task alone," insisted the official. "It was to keep the light burning. Everything else was secondary. There is no defense."

So it is with Paul's conclusion in the matter of running the race. We either run with perseverance to obtain the crown or we fall by the wayside in disgrace. We are given enough grace to finish our race. There will be a thousand distractions pulling at us from every side. Most will have worth of their own, but we are given a race to run. And running our race is really all that matters.

Let us run it well! I'll see you at the finish line!

Mileposts

What part does perseverance play in the Christian life?

_____
_____
_____
_____

Should we be "kicking the tires" when someone claims a relationship with Christ? Why? How?

_____
_____
_____
_____

What two sporting events does Paul use when he speaks of our perseverance?

_____
_____
_____
_____

What are the three main parts to running a race? How are all three interrelated?

_____
_____
_____
_____

What are some of the things that distract you from running your race with diligence?

_____

_____

_____

_____

How does your race affect the generation that follows you?

_____

_____

_____

_____

In what ways does the Holy Spirit build up your confidence levels as you run your race?

_____

_____

_____

_____

Paul uses the Greek word *adokimos* to describe the results of not finishing the race. What does this word mean?

_____

_____

_____

_____

NOTES

Chapter Seven

THE PRAYER-LIFE

The Christian life truly is of marvelous design. God has proven Himself to be the master designer as our lives unfold his plans for us. He said through the prophet Jeremiah, "For I know the thoughts that I think toward you, says the Lord, thoughts of peace and not of evil, to give you a future and a hope." (Jeremiah 29:11) God's plan for you cannot fail for it is based upon His own faithfulness.

Once God's plan is put into motion, He then lays out certain proofs that are irrefutable evidence that He is at work in your life. The greatest of these is that we continue in His plan despite our own inability to do so. He truly is the Author and the Finisher of what He has begun.

None of this would make much sense unless God revealed His purpose. Because He is Creator then He holds the sovereign right in determining exactly what the believer's purpose is. Of course, that purpose never violates His plan!

Incredibly, God arranges this deep and lasting relationship into a bond as deep as marriage itself. He describes us as the bride and His Son, Jesus Christ, as the Bridegroom. From this our passion serves as further evidence of His designing in our lives.

The Father not only sets into motion all of these details, but then makes sure that all of it will prosper. The believer can take comfort in this arrangement as it serves both God and us well. We can be sure of our welfare as believers when we see faith, love, and patience ever increasing in our daily living.

As our lives show more and more evidence of God's designing at work, we run the Christian race with discipline and diligence unto the very end. We finish well and one might conclude that is enough.

But wait!

God in His merciful designing has added one more detail that only He could have thought of and, furthermore, given the resources for this detail to succeed. As the Designer, He could have simply set all things into motion and stepped back into eternity to watch it all unfold. But we serve a gracious God who leaves nothing to chance.

In His divine wisdom He included an instrument which allows us as part of His designing to communicate directly with Him as the Designer. We never have to wonder or second guess at some detail. We never have to surrender in dismay when we just do not understand a certain feature of grace.

God has opened the portals of Heaven and bent His ear toward the children of His designing. He has given all believers the ability to speak directly with Him in prayer. This is the crowning element of His design. He is ready for His creation to approach Him and ask all things by faith in prayer.

This last element which I am including in the discussion of God's great design is not included last by accident. It is more a matter of avoidance on my part as the author. Each time I consider all of the pieces that are part of God's designing, my own deficiencies become self-evident. The greatest need I have in my life is prayer, yet I find myself seriously lacking in this matter.

With that off my proverbial chest, I am hoping that you can join me in a deeper desire to communicate with the Grand Designer Himself. What an amazing thought that God longs to hear from us in prayer!

This last chapter will include the following thoughts on prayer:

The Compulsion of Prayer
The Communication of Prayer
The Confidence of Prayer
The Confession of Prayer
The Need For Clarity in Prayer
The Confirmation of Answered Prayer

Much can be learned about prayer from simply studying the prayers that are so common in the Bible. Dr. Herbert Lockyer who wrote *All The Prayers of The Bible* has counted at least 650 prayers recorded in the Bible text. With this one subject so prominently included in the inspired scripture, one would conclude that we can glean vast riches by studying the text of these prayers.

With many choices to select from, I will use one of Daniel's prayers to lay the ground work for prayer in the life of the Christian. From the ninth chapter of Daniel's prophecy we can gather insight into the matter of prayer.

Daniel begins this portion of his writing by telling us that he was in captivity under the rule of the Chaldeans. He was studying the prophecy of Jeremiah when he began to understand that the 70 years of captivity was about to be concluded. This led him to pray the following:

"Then I set my face toward the Lord God to make request by prayer and supplications, with fasting, sackcloth, and ashes. And I prayed to the Lord my God, and made confession, and said, 'O Lord, great and awesome God, who keeps His covenant and mercy with those who love Him, and with those who keep His commandments, we have sinned and committed iniquity, we have done wickedly and rebelled, even by departing from Your precepts and Your judgments. Neither have we heeded Your servants the prophets, who spoke in Your name to our kings and our princes, to our fathers and all the people of the land. O Lord, righteousness belongs to You, but to us shame of face, as it is this day—to the men of Judah, to the inhabitants of Jerusalem and all Israel, those near and those far off in all the countries to which You have driven them, because of the unfaithfulness which they have committed against You.

O Lord, to us belongs shame of face, to our kings, our princes, and our fathers, because we have sinned against You. To the Lord our God belong mercy and forgiveness, though we have rebelled against Him. We have not obeyed the voice of the Lord our God, to walk in His laws, which He set before us by His servants the prophets. Yes, all Israel has transgressed Your law, and has departed so as not to obey Your voice; therefore the curse and the oath written in the Law of Moses the servant of God have been poured out on us, because we have sinned against Him. And He has confirmed His words, which He spoke against us and against our judges who judged us, by bringing upon us a great disaster; for under the whole heaven such has never been done as what has been done to Jerusalem.

As it is written in the Law of Moses, all this disaster has come upon us; yet we have not made our prayer before the Lord our God, that we might turn from our iniquities and understand Your truth. Therefore the Lord has kept the disaster in mind, and brought it upon us; for the Lord our God is righteous in all the works which He does, though we have not obeyed His voice. And now, O Lord our God, who brought Your people out of the land of Egypt with a mighty hand, and made Yourself a name, as it is this day—we have sinned, we have done wickedly!

O Lord, according to all Your righteousness, I pray, let Your anger and Your fury be turned away from Your city Jerusalem, Your holy mountain; because for our sins, and for the iniquities of our fathers, Jerusalem and Your people are a reproach to all those around us. Now therefore, our God, hear the prayer of Your servant, and his supplications, and for the Lord's sake cause Your face to shine on Your sanctuary, which is desolate. O my God, incline Your ear and hear; open Your eyes and see our desolations, and the city which is called by Your name; for we do not present our supplications before You because of our righteous deeds, but because of Your great mercies. O Lord, hear! O Lord, forgive! O Lord, listen and act! Do not delay for Your own sake, my God, for Your city and Your people are called by Your name.'" (Daniel 9:3-19)

It may seem a little extreme to include all of Daniel's prayer here as part of this chapter, but all of it is important in determining the evidence of prayer as vital to the Christian life. And, I do not think that you would want any part of one of your prayers deleted, would you? I didn't think so!

Now you have the context of Daniel's prayer. It was a desperate time; it was a dark time. Daniel needed answers from heaven to decipher what he had discovered in Jeremiah's prophecy. So it is with most of our prayers. They are offered many times as a last ditch effort after we have tried everything else. Yet, it is always prayer that begets an answer while we are in the pangs of despair.

We Find Ourselves Under A Compulsion to Pray

Someone said that we pray best when we pray out of the depths. Problems have a way of driving us to our knees. As Daniel began his prayer he laid out the problem clearly before the Lord. He did not try to hide from God what was evident in the lives of Israel.

He prayed, "we have sinned and committed iniquity, we have done wickedly and rebelled, even by departing from Your precepts and Your judgments. Neither have we heeded Your servants the prophets, who spoke in Your name to our kings and our princes, to our fathers and all the people of the land." (Daniel 9:5-6)

Notice that this man Daniel who was noted for his faithfulness to pray even under penalty of the lion's den begins his prayer with a plural pronoun. He did not try to distance himself from the national sin of Israel. It was because he owned this sin as his own that he could pray with such passion.

He confessed a departure from the revealed word of God and a rejection of the prophets whom God had sent to forewarn Israel of the consequences of their sin. He placed the blame across a wide spectrum. He declared the kings and princes responsible, the generations that had preceded him as culpable, and all of the common folks who dwelt in the land blameworthy. The rebellion had permeated all of Israel.

How similar does this sound to the time we are living in today? As Christians, we can bear evidence of our relationship to Christ by bearing as our own the sins of the nation. Do not be afraid to say *we* when under the compulsion to pray. Especially when it is problems that drive us to our knees. It is too easy to place the blame on others and attempt to pray from a position of pseudo-holiness.

Remember, we tend to give praise when we are looking in the mirror and attribute blame when we are looking out of the window. Start with what you see in the mirror and it will put you on your knees quickly!

It seems clear that the church and Christians in particular are not under much compulsion to pray in our day. One needs only visit a mid-week service in most of churches to reach this conclusion. If you can find a prayer meeting, it is usually some few minutes tacked onto the end of a Bible study or some other activity. There is little concerted effort to approach heaven with a sense of compulsion to pray.

It is not that we do not have our share of problems or sins for that matter. It is clearly a decision on our part to discount the impact that prayer could have in our lives as Christians. There was a day when the prayer meeting was of vital importance in the life of the church.

One such occasion has been recorded for our consideration. The prayer meeting was held on a Wednesday evening and the date was October 7, 1857. The pastor of the church was Charles Spurgeon. England was in dire straits with a war raging in faraway India. **This prayer meeting had over 6000 in attendance.**

Spurgeon's prayer holds closely to the format of Daniel's prayer. Here is the text of that prayer. Read it slowly and let it soak in one word and one phrase at a time. You will find few prayers offered today in this format.

"O God, the God of heaven and of earth, we do this day pay Thee reverence, and meekly bow our heads in adoration before Thine awful throne. We are the creatures of Thine hand; Thou hast made us, and not we ourselves. It is but just and right that we should pay unto Thee our adoration.

O God we are met together in a vast congregation for a purpose which demands all the power of piety, and all the strength of prayer. Send down Thy Spirit upon Thy servant, that he, whilst trembling in weakness, may be made strong to preach Thy Word, to lead forth this people in holy prayer, and to help them in that humiliation for which this day is set apart.

Come, O God, we beseech Thee; bow our hearts before Thee; instead of sackcloth and ashes give us true repentance, and hearts meekly reverent; instead of the outward guise, to which some pay their only homage, give us the inward spirit; and may we really pray, really humiliate ourselves, and really tremble before the Most High God.

Sanctify this service; make it useful unto us and honorable to Thyself. And O Thou dread Supreme, unto Thee shall be the glory and the honor, world without end. Amen."

Oh, God give us a compulsion to prayer like the prophets and preachers of old! We may be in a new day, but our problems and sins are just as familiar as they were to our forefathers.

It is not problems alone that should compel us to pray. If that were the case then we should only pray *for* problems instead of praying because of them. We also can be compelled to pray by the promises of God.

It is the assurance of God's promises that allows us to approach His throne with boldness (Hebrews 10:19). It is the fact of our close relationship to the Father that we can seek His face on the basis of those promises (Ephesians 2:6).

Jim Elliot, a missionary slain by the Auca Indians in the 1950's, once said, "God is still on His throne and man is still on his footstool. There's only a knees distance in between." Only a man both knowing his position in Christ and trusting in God's promises could make such a statement. Only a man who stands upon those promises could make such a statement in the face of any problem including being martyred for the faith!

Daniel calls upon God in prayer using three promises as he does so. He speaks these promises to God in the course of his prayer and in a fashion reminds God of His own attributes. In verses 7 and 14 he speaks of God's righteousness. In verse 9 he recounts God's mercy and forgiveness.

These attributes of God prove that God is not some idol who cannot respond to the prayers of His people. God does not simply act right, act in mercy, or offer forgiveness. He is righteous altogether; He is mercy manifested; He is forgiveness enforced.

On the same night that Spurgeon offered the invocation noted above, he went on to expound upon Daniel 9. He told the overflowing crowd, "We need not come before implacable deities who delight in the blood of the creatures whom it is pretended that they have made." Our prayers are not offered in hopes of appeasement, but in the assurance of appropriation. We expect God will do the right thing and do so according to His own character of mercy and forgiveness.

The actions of God are indeed based upon the justice required by His righteousness, but more than bringing about a just decision, God simply does what is right. This can bolster our compulsion to prayer because we know that whatever our situation is God will do right by us. It may not be exactly what *we* thought was right, but remember that His ways and thoughts are beyond ours (Romans 11:33).

Furthermore, His response to our prayers will not be based upon our past actions that may or may not have gotten us into the predicament we find ourselves. Daniel clearly noted that the children of Israel were filled with public shame because they had rebelled against His law. Even with this knowledge of past failures, Daniel still called upon God's mercy and forgiveness as promises that would resolve the problems they were facing.

Whether it is problems, promises, or both that drive us to our knees, prayer will always be a strong piece of evidence that we are Christians. Where others might run from God or foolishly blame Him for their circumstances, the believer will seek His face in prayer. This brings us to the second element involved in our prayer life: communication.

We Find Ourselves In Need Of Communication In Prayer

In this world of instant communication we are almost overwhelmed with information. Other than a few remote places you can reach out and touch anyone with just a few clicks upon your virtual keypad. As a matter of fact, we expect others to respond rapidly when we have attempted communication with them. Be it by voice, text, or even some visual method, we are frustrated when all we get is voice mail. It's like we are saying, "You know it's me and I'm important—so—PICK UP THE PHONE ALREADY!"

Prayer is just as instantaneous and there are absolutely no "dead spots." You can engage the God of the universe in a full blown conversation 24/7. You will never, ever get a busy signal or voice mail. But you may have experienced a time when you have approached Heaven's throne with a careless or pious attitude. Just as we do with our modern pieces of technology, we bow our heads to pray and say, "You know it's me and I'm important—so—PICK UP THE PRAYERLINE ALREADY!"

As Daniel prepared to reach out to God in prayer, he prepared himself for the encounter. Daniel describes his preparation in this manner: "Then I set my face toward the Lord God to make request by prayer and supplications, with fasting, sackcloth, and ashes." (Daniel 9:3)

Four things are evident as we look at Daniel's preparation for prayer: concentration, sincerity, admission of necessity, and humility. I do not see very much of this in most prayer meetings. Honestly, I do not see much of these preparations in my own life either...how about you?

Daniel began by setting his face toward the Lord God. This action showed that he was committing himself completely to the matter at hand. To set one's face instills the idea of framing the subject.

Frames are important not only for holding our photos or pictures securely in place, but also because a frame forces the observer to focus on that which is being framed. Daniel was saying that he was framing God into a focused point of reference. Literally, nothing was going to distract him from communicating with God.

If you have ever been paying only half attention to a child as they are speaking, you might have been brought into their focus when they reached out and turned your face toward theirs. This is the idea here. Daniel was focused in deepest concentration upon the subject of his communication with God. He had a request to ask of God. He did not need to turn God's face toward his. Instead, it was he who needed to concentrate and frame out the world while he sought the One who could fulfill his request.

To this heightened level of concentration Daniel added fasting. This is a concept that many Christians (especially in America) know little about in the 21st century. The very idea of going any period of time without eating is living an extreme life of faith to most and just plain weird to others. We have convinced ourselves in a land of plenty that self-denial when it comes to food is ludicrous. Only fanatics would go to such lengths in their prayer life, right?

Well, it just may be that we are not seeing more answers to our prayers because we have not added the element of sincerity. Fasting is not a foreign subject when you study the Bible for sure and it has not been many years ago that presidents and leaders of our own country called the nation to a time of prayer and fasting.

Unfortunately, we are in the business of creating prayer-free zones in America today. Actually our nation has bowed to the god of political correctness and bought into the idea that prayer should never be exercised outside of the confines of the church. God help us all if Christians were to begin fasting in concert with praying! If prayer alone can offend to such a degree, surely fasting on top of prayer would deem us as truly radical!

I heard about a sign in a principal's office (one of the prayer-free zones we have allowed to be created) that read: "In the event of nuclear attack, fire, or earthquake, the ban on prayer is temporarily lifted." That about says it all! We have relegated prayer to the status of a flare the we carry in the trunk of our vehicle. We have no intent of ever using it, but if an emergency of sufficient amplitude occurs we can pull it out, set it ablaze, and hope beyond all belief that help might come—someday!

Daniel's praying was not of flare-like quality. Focusing upon the only God who could both hear and answer, he was moved to a deepened level of sincerity. This prompted him to fast as he prayed about Israel's fallen condition.

Fasting should never become an activity in and of itself. Neither should fasting be seen as some sort of leverage in which you hope to convince God to move in your favor. It is fasting that deepens the sincerity of the believer and thereby brings us into greater focus upon the will of God.

It was the Pharisees who made an "art" of fasting. They wanted it to be regular and of renown in its function. It was so public that everyone knew what days, what length, and how deep their suffering was as they carried it out religiously (Matthew 6:16).

It is to be noted that Jesus told his disciples that there are times that the answer will only be discovered when both prayer and fasting are involved. The disciples had been approached by a father whose son was beset with epilepsy. The disciples could not help this man and he reported their failure to Jesus.

After Jesus healed the father's son, the disciples asked why they failed bring to pass the miracle needed. Jesus' response demonstrates the importance of fasting and its direct connection in praying through difficult situations.

"So Jesus said to them, 'Because of your unbelief; for assuredly, I say to you, if you have faith as a mustard seed, you will say to this mountain, 'Move from here to there,' and it will move; and nothing will be impossible for you. However, this kind does not go out except by prayer and fasting.'" (Matthew 17:19-21)

I can tell you that I have taken part in many forms of fasting and have fasted for up to 40 days. I did not die since I am writing this book at this very moment! All of us fast for a few hours each day. Remember the first meal of the day is called breakfast. It's a compound word: break—fast.

This book is not a treatise on the subject of fasting. I would recommend that you find some good material to read on the subject and prepare yourself for a level of sincerity in your prayer life that you most likely have never experienced.

Here are a few good resources that might enlighten you on the subject:

A Hunger for God: Desiring God through Fasting and Prayer
by John Piper

Beginner's Guide to Fasting
by Elmer Towns

The Power of Prayer and Fasting
by Ronnie Floyd

Always seek the Lord's guidance if you take this step in your prayer life. Of course, you must be sure that you are physically capable of fasting. Diseases such as diabetes may prevent fasting or cause a restricted form of fasting. Remember foremost that fasting is a matter of the heart. It is not a production to put on display nor is it some massive demonstration of will power. God will clearly direct when you should fast and when to break your fast.

The next step Daniel took in his deepening prayer life was the wearing of sackcloth. I can hear the groans already as you read this! Don't worry, I'm not about to inform you that your wardrobe is changing for the worse!

The wearing of sackcloth was a symbol of one's deep poverty. Sackcloth was the common dress of the mourner. When a person was seen wearing clothes made of nothing more than feed sacks, it was apparent that the person was in a deep state of contrition.

The outerwear demonstrated the great need that was being felt inwardly. As in a mourner's life, there was a sense of unbearable loss.

We will never be fully engaged in our prayer life as a believer until we reach some point of necessity that can only be filled if God answers us. We finally get to the place where all of our resources are consumed, the arm of flesh is of no avail, and only heaven's bounty can meet our need.

Daniel's choice to wear sackcloth was to place upon his flesh a rough material that would have caused itching and irritation. The sackcloth would be worn until there was an answer.

Just as the hunger pangs brought on by fasting would serve as a ready reminder to pray, the itching and rash of sackcloth would cause the wearer to cry out to the point of desperation for deliverance.

Once again, the sackcloth was not some charm used to convince God to answer. The sackcloth served as a prompting to those who may have been previously at ease in Zion.

Prayer has a unique way of getting us out of our comfort zones. The prayer that shakes heaven and changes things here on earth will never be of the Now-I-Lay-Me-Down-To-Sleep variety. Prayer that moves heaven will make not only the one praying uncomfortable, but it will make the world around him itch with excitement!

Begin now to admit your necessity. Get uncomfortable in your present state and seek God's face with such sincerity that the rest of the world is out of the frame of your vision. At this point you are well on your way to your first real session of prayer. You will find yourself kneeling with Daniel in intercession for your Israel!

Daniel concludes the preparation to prayer by mentioning that he covered himself in ashes. Where fasting serves as a symbol of sincerity and sackcloth pictures our desperate need, ashes portray absolute humility.

Humility is not a natural act for us as humans. Pride comes much easier. It is possible to be very proud of just how humble you are trying to be! Charles Spurgeon said of pride in our prayers, "Proud prayers may knock their heads on mercy's lintel, but they can never pass through the portal. You cannot expect anything of God unless you put yourself in the right place, that is, as a beggar at his footstool; then will he hear you, and not until then." He went on to say, "To stoop well is a grand art in prayer."

As sackcloth was in a time of mourning, ashes were used in these times as well. The use of ashes had a much broader use than mourning alone. When a person covered themselves with ashes it was a token of self-abhorrence. It served as a way to hide or disguise one's outward appearance. The ash covered person was in essence saying, "I cannot bear to look upon my own appearance. I am ashamed of what I have become."

Now this flies in the face (no pun intended) of many today who only speak of self-worth and making sure that everyone gets their fair shake. Humility is a very scarce commodity in most people's lives. Unfortunately, it is not found very often in the lives of Christians either.

Humility is an attribute that is necessary if we are to come before God in desperate times. James said in his epistle, "But He gives more grace. Therefore He says: 'God resists the proud, but gives grace to the humble.'" (James 4:6) James quotes in this verse the wisdom of Solomon from Proverbs. Surely the wisest man who ever lived knew what he was speaking of when it came to humility. He had discovered that pride always goes before the fall as he left humility in the dust of his life and was filled with pride.

Solomon's vast knowledge left him with a sense of life being filled with vanity. He repeats this theme throughout Ecclesiastes. John Lange wrote in *A Commentary on the Holy Scriptures: Ecclesiastes*, "But because knowledge easily puffeth up (1 Cor. 8:1), wise and learned men have so much greater need to beg God to keep them in true humility."

Remember that Daniel and his three Hebrew friends were set aside early on in the captivity because of their remarkable wisdom. Daniel was an interpreter of dreams. He had known what it was to have a direct word from God. Yet in this occasion, he sought the Lord in prayer with humility.

The words of a 17th century Frenchman named François Fenelon summarizes my thoughts on Daniel's preparation to prayer very well.

Tell God all that is in your heart, as one unloads one's heart, it's pleasures, and it's pains, to a dear friend.

Tell him your troubles, that he may comfort you; tell him your joys, that he may sober them; tell him your longings, that he may purify them; tell him your dislikes, that he may help you conquer them; talk to him of your temptations, that he may shield you from them; show him the wounds of your heart, that he may heal them; lay bare your indifference to good, your depraved tastes for evil, your instability. Tell him how self-love makes you unjust to others, how vanity tempts you to be insincere, how pride disguises you to yourself and others.

If you thus pour out your weaknesses, needs, troubles, there will be no lack of what to say. You will never exhaust the subject. It is continually being renewed. People who have no secrets from each other never want for subject of conversation. They do not weigh their words, for there is nothing to be held back, neither do they seek for something to say. They talk out of the abundance of their heart, without consideration they say just what they think.

Blessed are they who attain to such familiar, unreserved intercourse with God.

We Need To Have Confidence In Our Prayers

The *Concise Oxford English Dictionary* defines the word "confidence" as:

1. the belief that one can have faith in or rely on someone or something.

2. the telling of private matters or secrets with mutual trust.

Both of these definitions provide insight into the need for confidence in our prayer life. Without confidence, prayer would be at the least an exercise filled with insecurity and at the most frustratingly filled with indecision. We simply could not pray if we did not have faith that Someone was listening or that we could pray with total assurance that our prayers were just between God and us.

How can we be sure that both of these qualities are present in the God to whom we direct our prayers? Daniel gives us evidence in his prayer as recorded in Daniel 9. "And I prayed to the Lord my God, and made confession, and said, "O Lord, great and awesome God, who keeps His covenant and mercy with those who love Him, and with those who keep His commandments…" (Daniel 9:4)

The first evidence that Daniel gives us as a confidence builder is the fact that we pray to a God whose character is beyond question. Daniel sought audience with a great and awesome God.

The word great is not fully fathomed in the English language. It is just a measurement used to compare one item to another. In its simplest form it is an adjective which means that something is above average. It is used sometimes in excitement and sometimes in exasperation. For example: "We are going on a vacation!" and your response might be, "Great!" On another occasion you hear a report that your car has been stolen and you cry out, "Oh, great!"

Daniel's use of the term great is best explained as it is connected to the word awesome. The Hebrew word reveals a view of God that He was out of the ordinary, beyond degree, higher in magnitude, and tremendous in effect.

The fact that our prayers are offered to a GREAT God gives us confidence that we can never ask anything that is beyond His ability to perform. In Mark's gospel the account of the rich, young ruler is told. The young man comes to Christ seeking the way to eternal life. With a false sense of accomplishment on his part, Jesus commands him to sell all that he has and follow him.

The young man goes away sad because he cannot part with his wealth. Jesus looks at his disciples and tells them, "'How hard it is for those who have riches to enter the kingdom of God!' And the disciples were astonished at His words. But Jesus answered again and said to them, 'Children, how hard it is for those who trust in riches to enter the kingdom of God! It is easier for a camel to go through the eye of a needle than for a rich man to enter the kingdom of God.'" (Mark 10:23-25)

The disciples were astonished at Jesus' remarks and questioned who could ever be saved. Jesus answered their concerns with a confidence building word on the character of God. "With men it is impossible, but not with God; for with God all things are possible." (Mark 10:27) God's greatness is beyond compare for there is nothing that is beyond His ability.

But Daniel adds the word awesome to his description of God's character. Awesome is another adjective used to describe God, but it really defines Daniel's and our response to the greatness of God more than it does God's character. God is awesome, but only as we respond to Him in awe. We see Him as awesome when we are filled with reverential fear in His presence. His awesomeness is the box which contains our reaction to His greatness!

We live in a world that has taken the word awesome and lowered it to the temporal and transitory. Awesome is used to define how we feel about stuff that really does not matter in the grand scheme of things. I hear the word awesome used to describe the most mundane of things, most of which are of fleeting quality. There is no reverential fear, but rather some gleeful response to a tickling of our fancy.

I would implore you to reserve the use of the word awesome for God alone. For it is He alone that will both hear and answer your need in prayer. Let the word awesome contain your response to the greatness of God and you will never see God as the "upstairs butler" who must run to answer the bell you ring in prayer. You will see a God who can make all things possible. You will see a God who can and will answer. He is not some God who is not great (the double negative serves well here)! Our God is a GREAT and AWESOME God!

The Psalmist summarized the great awesomeness of God very well in these verses from Psalm 115:1-8:

Not unto us, O Lord, not unto us,
But to Your name give glory,
Because of Your mercy,
Because of Your truth.

Why should the Gentiles say,
"So where is their God?"

But our God is in heaven;
He does whatever He pleases.

Their idols are silver and gold,
The work of men's hands.

They have mouths, but they do not speak;
Eyes they have, but they do not see;

They have ears, but they do not hear;
Noses they have, but they do not smell;

They have hands, but they do not handle;
Feet they have, but they do not walk;
Nor do they mutter through their throat.

Those who make them are like them;
So is everyone who trusts in them.

Now, back to our definitions of confidence. The first definition related to trust in someone's character. The second takes into account a trust that is of mutual quality to the point that private and secret matters might be fully shared.

Daniel uses a term that speaks of this heightened level of confidence. He tells us that God is a covenant keeping God. This quality of relationship to God in prayer cannot be taken lightly. You will never truly open your life to God in prayer until you come to the place of trusting Him in covenant.

You see, our problem is not with God failing to keep His part of the covenant. We are the ones that fall so short in the promise department. Time and again we make promises and without fail—WE FAIL!

When Daniel brings up God's covenant keeping he is purposefully setting the stage for the rest of his prayer. He knows that Israel has failed to keep their end of the covenant relationship they had with God. The very fact of their captivity was a direct consequence of their failure to keep the commands of God.

They had refused to keep the law of the Sabbath as it related to the land. Refusing to let the land lie fallow once every seven years for a period that spanned 490 years, God had removed them from the Promised Land. They were forced into captivity that had lasted for 70 years. Divide 490 by 70 and you get the number seven. God was claiming the Sabbath that was due in his covenant relationship with Israel.

It was Daniel's study of Jeremiah's prophecy about this 70 year captivity that drove him to his knees in prayer. He knew that Israel was guilty, yet he engaged God in prayer.

How unlike us is this? When we find ourselves under the strain of guilt, we often times run from God. We refuse to communicate with Him and instead go into the captivity of our own unfaithfulness and prayerlessness.

Daniel was not dismissing the guilt of Israel or himself. He simply was placing at the forefront the covenant keeping promises of God. In essence, he was reminding God of His own words. Not that God needed to be reminded, instead, the reminder was in effect a recalling of the assurance that God would never forsake His own promise to the children of Abraham.

God had made several covenants with men both individually and cooperatively throughout the history and context of the Bible. Two of these covenants stand out as significant and surely were on Daniel's mind as he began his prayer.

God had made a covenant with David that there would always be one of his heirs upon the throne of Israel. That covenant will ultimately be fulfilled when Christ sits upon the throne to rule from Jerusalem. The second covenant actually came first as it preceded the Davidic covenant by at least 1000 years. It was the Abrahamic covenant.

This covenant promised that the children of Abraham would be innumerable as the stars in the sky or the sand upon the seashore. God then promised Abraham that the land where he now dwelled would be his forever. God sealed this covenant with Abraham in an unusual way. This account is recorded in Genesis 15.

Abraham believed God (Genesis 15:6), but he asked how he could know all of this for sure. It was at this point that God engaged Abraham in a covenant arrangement.

"And he said, 'Lord God, how shall I know that I will inherit it?' So He said to him, 'Bring Me a three-year-old heifer, a three-year-old female goat, a three-year-old ram, a turtledove, and a young pigeon.' Then he brought all these to

Him and cut them in two, down the middle, and placed each piece opposite the other; but he did not cut the birds in two." (Genesis 15:8-11)

This scene is a bit strange to us in our day, but this would not have appeared as abnormal to Abraham. When two people sought to come to an agreement or covenant in Abraham's day, just such an arrangement would be made.

The animals would be killed and divided in a similar fashion. The parties making the covenant would then walk together hand in hand along the pathway marked by the severed carcasses. The promise made while walking this pathway would be sealed and the consequences of breaking the covenant would be symbolized by the divided bodies of the animals. Literally the two would agree that breaking their agreement would result in consequences similar to what had happened to the animals which bordered the pathway of their covenant agreement.

It was at this point that God did something totally contrary to the custom of that day. "Now when the sun was going down, a deep sleep fell upon Abram; and behold, horror and great darkness fell upon him. — And it came to pass, when the sun went down and it was dark, that behold, there appeared a smoking oven and a burning torch that passed between those pieces. (Genesis 15:11;17)

God in His omniscience did not rely upon Abraham to keep his end of the bargain. Appearing as a smoking oven and a burning torch, He walked the pathway alone. He made the covenant with Abraham and secured the keeping thereof upon His own character. Abraham's faithfulness or unfaithfulness carried no weight in the culmination of the covenant. It was all based upon the unchangeable character of God.

This covenant keeping quality of God's nature assures that we can approach God in prayer no matter what our past failures might be. Daniel ties God's mercy closely to His covenant keeping. We, like Daniel, can thank God at the very beginning of our prayers for His mercy being available and that He never will forsake His covenant to us.

We have the basis of a covenant given to us as Jesus prayed in John 17:20-23 "I do not pray for these alone, but also for those who will believe in Me through their word; that they all may be one, as You, Father, are in Me, and I in You; that they also may be one in Us, that the world may believe that You sent Me. And the glory which You gave Me I have given them, that they may be one just as We are one: I in them, and You in Me; that they may be made perfect in one, and that the world may know that You have sent Me, and have loved them as You have loved Me."

You and I can be fully confident in our prayer life because God is who He is. We do not pray with confidence based upon our covenant keeping abilities. We do not pray to such a great and awesome God from a position of perfection, but instead we see the greatness of God and that exposes the grossness of our sin.

Finding ourselves in this predicament, we can only call upon His mercy in our time of need and go with confidence before our covenant keeping God who loves us as He loved His only begotten Son. Now that's awesome!

We Need Confession in Our Prayers

When I first became a believer I followed a very simple process of praying using the acrostic ACTS. It stood for adoration, confession, thanksgiving, and supplication. It served as a good guide for praying through a lot of things.

I do not think that some particular order is necessary for us to follow in our prayer life, but it is interesting that Daniel followed somewhat of an order that follows the ACTS model. Confession of sin came very early in his prayer for Israel and himself.

Where confession follows immediately upon the heels of adoration in the ACTS model, confession is preceded by a need for confidence in Daniel's model. As always, the Holy Spirit directing the pen of the writer has given us a principle that we can use to fashion our own prayer lives.

If confession is to be made, as it should be, we really do need to know that we have an audience with the only One who can truly forgive and cleanse us from our sin. This high level of confidence then gives us assurance as we include a time of confession in our prayers.

Daniel's description of the awesomeness of God serves as a spotlight upon the condition of the people. The more we see God's greatness—the more we see the grossness of our own sin. The brighter God's glory shines—the darker sin appears to us.

Jerry Oliver is an evangelist that I have known for many years. He and his team travelled across the country in a converted passenger bus. The miles sometimes left the bus in less than optimum condition and it failed to carry them to their destination from time to time.

On one such occasion the bus broke down on the side of the interstate. Jerry sent his team on to their destination and he remained with bus attempting to make some of the repairs. As night fell, he retired for some much needed rest.

In the dimness of the battery operated lights he washed his face and went to sleep for the night. The next morning in the light of a new day, he looked into the mirror and was amazed. Where spots of grease and dirt had been upon his face from the attempted repairs, he now saw his face fully covered with grime. He had not removed the dirt in the dim light. He had simply spread it evenly over his entire face! Only in the fullness of the light could he recognize his uncleanness.

This is exactly what happens to us when we pray. As we enter into the fullness of God's presence, we begin to see more clearly our own sinful condition. This is what we see in Daniel's prayer.

"O Lord, righteousness belongs to You, but to us shame of face, as it is this day—to the men of Judah, to the inhabitants of Jerusalem and all Israel, those near and those far off in all the countries to which You have driven them, because of the unfaithfulness which they have committed against You. O Lord, to us belongs shame of face, to our kings, our princes, and our fathers, because we have sinned against You." (Daniel 9:7-8) Daniel picks up this theme again in verses 16 and 17, "O Lord, according to all Your righteousness, I pray, let Your anger and Your fury be turned away from Your city Jerusalem, Your holy mountain; because for our sins, and for the iniquities of our fathers, Jerusalem and Your people are a reproach to all those around us. Now therefore, our God, hear the prayer of Your servant, and his supplications, and for the Lord's sake cause Your face to shine on Your sanctuary, which is desolate."

Notice that Daniel did not try to isolate himself from the need for confession. He used plural pronouns as he prayed. Over and again he speaks of *our* sin, *we* have sinned, and to *us* belongs shame. Whether Daniel was as guilty as all of Israel is immaterial at this point. He was praying for the nation of which he was a part and he knew that the consequences of cooperate or national sin affects all. It affects those who are sinning, those they live among, and even other nations and neighbors. Truly, this is what we see happening in America!

As believers we can no longer sit idly by and assume that we will not suffer the effects of judgment by God. We must begin to pray for ourselves, our neighbors, our country, and yes, even the world. The scripture is plain: "For everyone to whom much is given, from him much will be required; and to whom much has been committed, of him they will ask the more." (Luke 12:48) We have been given so much more than the rest of the world combined. We will be held accountable!

Four insights can be gained from studying the confessional portion of Daniel's prayer. First, he uses the word sin without disclaimer. Sin is an act or feeling that transgresses something forbidden or ignores something required by God's law or character; whether in thought, feeling, speech, or action. Sin is without excuse since the law of God is written upon our hearts.

The Apostle Paul declares this in such a way that none are left with an excuse. "For as many as have sinned without law will also perish without law, and as many as have sinned in the law will be judged by the law (for not the hearers of the law are just in the sight of God, but the doers of the law will be justified; for when Gentiles, who do not have the law, by nature do the things in the law, these, although not having the law, are a law to themselves, who show the work of the law written in their hearts, their conscience also bearing witness, and between themselves their thoughts accusing or else excusing them) in the day when God will judge the secrets of men by Jesus Christ, according to my gospel." (Romans 2:12-16)

We must come before God with our sins fully exposed. This is especially necessary as believers if we are to maintain our fellowship in Christ. "If we say that we have no sin, we deceive ourselves, and the truth is not in us. If we confess our sins, He is faithful and just to forgive us our sins and to cleanse us from all unrighteousness. If we say that we have not sinned, we make Him a liar, and His word is not in us. (1 John 1:8-10)

What are the consequences of our sin when it is left unchecked and unconfessed? We see in Daniel's prayer that the remaining three insights gained are directly connected to the sin of Israel. They are: shame, separation, and scorn.

The sin and ultimately the unfaithfulness of Israel had brought to them what Daniel called "shame of face." What does this phrase mean?

Shame is an a negative emotion that combines feelings of dishonor, unworthiness, and embarrassment. It usually is revealed first and foremost in the facial features of a person. The head will be dropped and the eyes downcast. There may even be a discoloration of the skin in response to being ashamed.

The Hebrew word *bôsheth* is translated as shame. The word has a fuller meaning than mere embarrassment. The Hebrew reader would understand that the shame was a result of disappointment and confusion. Scripture tells us that God is not the author of confusion (1 Corinthians 14:33) and that hope based upon the love of God will never produce shame (Romans 5:5). Therefore, shame of face was a result of Israel departing from the truth of God which brought about confusion and they had lost their hope in God's love which left them ashamed before God and their neighbors.

When sin is left unconfessed it always leads to isolation and separation. First, we are separated from God and then from everyone else. Daniel said, "Now therefore, our God, hear the prayer of Your servant, and his supplications, and for the Lord's sake cause Your face to shine on Your sanctuary, which is desolate." (Daniel 9:17)

It is very easy to see the effects of unconfessed sin today in our land. The churches are desolated. The believers are not attending and the unbelievers are not seeking a place to find God. In both cases, unconfessed sin is leaving the sanctuary of God empty.

The idea of desolation to Daniel was one of astonishment brought about by utter ruin; to be stunned by the condition of destruction. We are happy to claim that God will show up if two or three are gathered in His name, but I am not so sure of this. We are commanded to gather as believers…"not forsaking the assembling of ourselves together, as is the manner of some, but exhorting one another, and so much the more as you see the Day approaching." (Hebrews 10:25)

We are to be ready to give an answer to all who are seeking answers about the God we serve. "But sanctify the Lord God in your hearts, and always be ready to give a defense to everyone who asks you a reason for the hope that is in you, with meekness and fear;" (1 Peter 3:15) It's very difficult to withstand the onslaught of the world and to answer their questions when you are unfaithful in attendance and share in the desolation of God's house.

Finally, we must never be part of the world's scorn for God. Scorn means to hold in derision or have contempt for someone or something. Unfortunately, the world's idea about God has come directly from us.

Daniel said that all the people around them were holding Jerusalem (the holy city of God) and Israel (God's holy people) in open reproach. The idea here is that of being laid bare. Israel was fully exposed by their unconfessed sin. They had been stripped naked before the world. They were no longer reflecting the character of the God they claimed to know.

Some would say that confession is good for the soul and I would agree that it is. Our minds, wills, and emotions are all part of our souls and are all affected by unconfessed sin. But we need not forget that unconfessed sin affects much more than us personally. All who we come into contact with on a daily basis are directly influenced by our confession or lack thereof. We are in this sense truly our brother's keeper.

Let the world's opinion of God never be impacted by your unconfessed sin. As we are made right vertically, we are made right horizontally. Both a vertical and horizontal beam are used to make a cross. Let your acquaintances always see both parts at work in your life.

We Need Clarity In Our Prayer Life

There is nothing more frustrating than unclear instructions. It could be that the instructions have not been articulated distinctly or that the instructions are of such detailed length that they have lost their capacity to elucidate. Either way the intended results are usually thwarted and mistakes are made.

When it comes to prayer clarity is important—not for God's sake, but for ours. He has no problem discerning what we mean. Actually, he knows the thoughts and intents of the heart (Hebrews 4:12-13).

The clarity of our prayer life will take on three dimensions. It will be directed. It will be dependent. It will be definite.

It is very clear from Daniel's words that his prayer was not just flippantly thrown up toward the gates of heaven. It was not offered with a holy-hope-so. It was issued in faith as he sought God's face in a time of great need.

His prayer was directed toward a God in whom he had a personal relationship. It is only at this deep level that he could use the pronoun "my." "O *my* God, incline Your ear and hear; open Your eyes and see our desolations, and the city which is called by Your name; for we do not present our supplications before You because of our righteous deeds, but because of Your great mercies. O Lord, hear! O Lord, forgive! O Lord, listen and act! Do not delay for Your own sake, *my* God, for Your city and Your people are called by Your name." (Daniel 9:18-19, *emphasis mine*)

He was seeking an audience with the God of the universe. He implored God to open His ears to hear and His eyes to see. Remember previously we talked about the fact that Israel had been laid bare before the world. Now Daniel is asking God to see the barrenness of the nation. He tells God that the basis of his prayer is not one of righteousness on the part of him or his people, but because of God's great mercies.

He then repeats three times the name of the one to whom he is directing his prayer. He says, "O Lord, hear! O Lord, forgive! O Lord, listen and act!" He declares that the One on the other end of his prayers is none other than *Adonai*. This name of God means sovereign, controller, or master. The predicament of Israel was such that only the Ruler of All would be able to help them.

Daniel's prayer declared his dependence upon God. He declares that we are *Your* people and that this is *Your* city. Furthermore, he prays that Israel was a people called by *Your* name. This declaration of dependence had a two-fold purpose. First, it stated without equivocation that Daniel did not expect help from anyone else other than God Himself. Second, it served as a reminder to God that they were after all *His* people.

Dependence in prayer is not possible unless the person praying knows God intimately and that He will not fail to keep all of His promises. You simply would never rely upon God in this manner unless He could be trusted implicitly. David Case and David Holdren spoke of trusting God in their book, *1-2 Peter, 1-3 John, Jude: a Commentary for Bible Students*, "The true Christian attitude is not self-abandonment or resignation, but it is a positive expression of bowing before God and trusting Him for everything in life. The reason for such action is because he cares (1 Peter 5:7) for the individual believer. This verb to care means there is a constant care and concern for the individual on God's part."

Our dependence upon God as we pray grows as we learn by experience that He can always be trusted. David sang of this in the Psalms: "Our fathers trusted in You; they trusted, and You delivered them. They cried to You, and were delivered; they trusted in You, and were not ashamed." (Psalms 22:4-5)

These verses include all of the concepts of confidence, confessing, and clarity. David speaks of the trust of the fathers. Herein is the idea of confidence in God's provision. This resulted in them not being ashamed or embarrassed which produced a great hope. This then led to a deeper dependence upon God in David's present predicament.

Finally, Daniel demonstrated the definitive quality of his prayer. He asked God to intercede for His own sake. The concept of God's sake is tied closely to His purpose. Daniel asked that all of His prayer be answered in accordance to God's supreme purpose.

It is this one definite reason that we can pray under all circumstances. God's purpose will never be undone or abandoned. For this very reason Paul could boldly say, "And we know that all things work together for good to those who love God, to those who are the called according to His purpose." (Romans 8:28)

The purpose of God is not being shaped by our circumstances. His purpose has always been in place and the circumstances under which we find ourselves existing are all working out for our good *according* to His purpose. This adds to our prayer life an assurance that prayer works not based on our ability to pray, but upon the one who defines our prayer!

This is why the prayer life of a believer is a sure piece of evidence in proving that we are indeed a Christian. The prayer life of Samuel F.B. Morse gives us insight into the importance of prayer in his life.

In an interview, George Hervey inquired of Morse, "Professor Morse, when you were making your experiments at the university, did you ever come to a standstill, not knowing what to do next?"

"I've never discussed this with anyone, so the public knows nothing about it. But now that you ask me, I'll tell you frankly—I prayed for more light."

"And did God give you the wisdom and knowledge you needed?"

"Yes He did," said Morse. "That's why I never felt I deserved the honors that came to me from America and Europe because of the invention associated with my name. I had made a valuable application of the use of electrical power, but it was all through God's help. It wasn't because I was superior to other scientists. When the Lord wanted to bestow this gift on mankind He had to use someone. I'm just grateful He chose to reveal it to me."

In view of these facts, it's not surprising that the inventor's first message over the telegraph was: "What hath God wrought!"

Truly Morse set out to do the impossible and sought to do it all for the sake of God alone. What has God wrought in your life that serves as the evidence He alone could be the source and supplier of the answer? It's all working itself out according to His purpose!

We Need Confirmation In Our Prayer Life

Living in a world of instant communication is not always all that it is cracked up to be. We are literally within reach of nearly everyone on a 24/7 basis. We expect—no, we demand a response to every call, every email, every text we make or send.

This creates a need in us for some sort of confirmation on the part of whoever we are attempting to reach. Of course, the assumption is always that they actually listened to our voicemail or read our written words. This is not always the case. Sometimes things just happen in this digital world that we have grown so accustomed to in the 21st century.

Voicemails are deleted and texts just are not delivered. Since we did our part in hitting the send button, we are expecting the recipient to confirm receipt. But again, things happen...

Not so with prayer!

We have an overwhelming assurance that when we pray the message is delivered. Not later today or tomorrow, but right now...faster than some computer on the other side of the world can respond to our command to send or request to read. Prayer is always heard immediately by God.

Now before you get too angry for not having received confirmation from heaven, we must properly define true prayer—not just words spoken or thought out, but wholly genuine prayer that catches the immediate attention of God.

Thankfully, the Bible gives us just such a definition. It is found in 1 John 5:14, "Now this is the confidence that we have in Him, that if we ask anything according to His will, He hears us." The confirmation of our prayer being heard by God is always found in the proposition that we have sent the prayer heavenward in accordance to His will.

If there were no other reason to discover God's will, then the confirmation of our prayer requests should be enough. We just cannot toss prayers about willy-nilly and expect that God must scurry about responding to our whims. The confirmation of our prayers being heard is asking inside the parameters of His will. You can ask anything that you please as long as it does not violate God's will. If it does not fit God's will for you, He simply will not respond.

God's will is discovered in several ways. First, we can read His Word, the Bible, and from there gather the information needed to discern His will. Second, we can determine God's will by the sense of peace that the Holy Spirit gives us about a particular matter. Third, we can consider the circumstances in which we find ourselves.

The first and second processes may be interchanged, but never allow circumstances to trump either of the first two ways of discovering God's will. Most of the time circumstances will lead us to ask God for things that simply do not conform to His will. In those cases, He will not reply.

The next verse in 1 John 5 confirms the fact that when God hears He always answers. "And if we know that He hears us, whatever we ask, we know that we have the petitions that we have asked of Him." (1 John 5:15)

So, we can have assurance of God hearing and answering. It is in the answer to prayer that we receive the greatest confirmation of all. Daniel received just such a confirmation while he was in the act of praying.

"Now while I was speaking, praying, and confessing my sin and the sin of my people Israel, and presenting my supplication before the Lord my God for the holy mountain of my God, yes, while I was speaking in prayer, the man Gabriel, whom I had seen in the vision at the beginning, being caused to fly swiftly, reached me about the time of the evening offering. And he informed me, and talked with me, and said, 'O Daniel, I have now come forth to give you skill to understand. At the beginning of your supplications the command went out, and I have come to tell you, for you are greatly beloved; therefore consider the matter, and understand the vision:'" (Daniel 9:20-23)

Remember from the beginning of this chapter that Daniel was driven to prayer because he had been studying the prophecies of Jeremiah concerning the time of Israel's captivity. All that has been discussed about prayer up to this point has led to the answer that Daniel sought.

His problems had driven him to his knees. He called upon God based upon the promises of God's word. He communicated with God openly and honestly as he assumed the sins of Israel to be his own. He was confident that God would answer because of God's character. He spoke with clarity as he directed his prayer to the ear of God alone. And now he had his confirmation! God sent Gabriel with a confirming answer.

Gabriel enlightened Daniel about the prophecies of Jeremiah, but then went even further to disclose God's calendar to the end of time. When you get into the position of asking according to God's will, you had better be ready. The answer just might be bigger than your asking.

So scripture tells us, "Now to Him who is able to do exceedingly abundantly above all that we ask or think, according to the power that works in us, to Him be glory in the church by Christ Jesus to all generations, forever and ever. Amen." (Ephesians 3:20-21)

Answered prayer is indeed a confirmation, but it is also a wonderful encouragement. Michael P. Green in *Illustrations for Biblical Preaching* gives a great illustration on how prayer works. "Prayer is much like a check to be countersigned by two parties. I sign the check and send it up to heaven. If Jesus Christ also signs it, it does not matter how large it is—it will be honored." When we ask and receive the answer we can be assured that we are living in the midst of God's will for our lives. Ask big! You can never bankrupt heaven!

When our prayers are answered there will always be an enlightenment. Suddenly, we will be able to discern how the hand of God was at work long before the answer was actually given. In Daniel chapter 10 the angel informs Daniel that the answer to his prayer had been on its way from the very beginning, but had been held up by the workings of Satan.

"Then he said to me, 'Do not fear, Daniel, for from the *first day that you set your heart to understand,* and to humble yourself before your God, your words were heard; and I have come because of your words. But the prince of the kingdom of Persia withstood me twenty-one days; and behold, Michael, one of the chief princes, came to help me, for I had been left alone there with the kings of Persia. Now I have come to make you understand what will happen to your people in the latter days, for the vision refers to many days yet to come.'" (Daniel 10:12-14 *emphasis mine*)

Sometimes when we grow a bit impatient in our prayer life, we need to be reminded that God is always at work. The assurance we have is that God always wins in the end! Never doubt the answer when the prayer is asked inside the parameters of God's will. Remember and faint not for we ought always to pray. "Rejoice always, pray without ceasing, in everything give thanks; for this is the will of God in Christ Jesus for you." (1 Thessalonians 5:16-18)

Prayer is indeed the crowning evidence for the Christian life. It is in our prayer life that we discover all the ways that we can be more assured of our relationship with the Living God of the universe.

We can be confident that God has a plan for us that supersedes time and space. Prayer will provide proof of our Christianity as it is evidenced in us continually walking in the faith and not being moved by every wind of doctrine. The purpose of the Christian life will be revealed through prayer as we live out God's will daily. Our passion will deepen as we seek God in prayer and discover anew that we love Him because he first loved us.

Our souls will prosper as our faith, love, and patience grows to levels we never thought possible before. As we run the race set before us, it will be through prayer that we find the strength to run to the end and then pass the baton to the generation that follows us.

It will not always be easy. We may have to live out our Christianity with debilitating problems and concerns. Paul had to live with his thorn in the flesh. John was never rescued from exile on the Isle of Patmos.

William Cowper lived a difficult life during the late 18th century. He suffered from severe depression and spent a short time in an asylum in England, the land of his birth. Out of this life which seemed to be shaped by unanswered prayer, he became a poet and wrote many hymns. Some of those include, "Oh For a Closer Walk with God," "God Moves in a Mysterious Way," and "There Is a Fountain Filled with Blood."

Several of his hymns were on the subject of prayer. It certainly seems that Cowper fully understood the importance of prayer in the Christian life.

The verses of one such hymn summarize well his convictions on prayer and serve in a most powerful way as the closing thoughts on this final evidence for the Christian life. Oh, that all Christians everywhere might find the hope that comes from praying until no one can deny your claim to a relationship with Jesus Christ as your Lord and Savior!

Prayer makes the darkest cloud withdraw;
Prayer climbs the ladder Jacob saw,
Gives exercise to faith and love,
Brings every blessing from above.

Restraining prayer, we cease to fight;
Prayer makes the Christian's armor bright;
And Satan trembles when he sees
The weakest saint upon his knees.

Have you no words? ah!, think again;
Words flow apace when you complain,
And fill the fellow-creature's ear
With the sad tale of all your care.

Were half the breath thus vainly spent,
To heaven in supplication sent,
Our cheerful song would oftener be,
"Hear what the Lord hath done for me!"

~WILLIAM COWPER~

Mileposts

How important is it to include prayer in our daily walk as a believer?

_____

_____

_____

_____

How are problems used to get us better into the position to pray earnestly?

_____

_____

_____

_____

Daniel prayed with the promises of God as the basis for his prayer. What were those promises? What promises are you basing your prayer life upon at this time?

_____

_____

_____

_____

Describe how fasting can be an integral part of your prayer life.

_____

_____

_____

_____

How does the author relate the use of sackcloth and ashes by Daniel to our prayer lives today?

_____
_____
_____
_____

How does God's character affect the content of your prayers?

_____
_____
_____
_____

Why is confession needed in your prayer life? How did Daniel include himself in the national sin of Israel?

_____
_____
_____
_____

The clarity of our prayer life will take on three dimensions. It will be _____.

It will be _____.

It will be _____.

How has God confirmed your prayer life through answered prayer? Write a brief testimony of answered prayer below.

_____

_____

_____

_____

_____

_____

_____

_____

_____

_____

_____

_____

_____

_____

_____

_____

_____

_____

_____

_____

_____

_____

_____

_____

_____

_____

_____

_____

_____

_____

_____

_____

_____

NOTES

Conclusion

The evidences for the Christian life as discussed in this book are not meant to be inclusive of all that could serve as confirmation of your belief in Jesus Christ as your Savior. I do believe that the six that make up the content of this study are some of the most important.

You may or may not find that all six of these evidences are present in your life or that they are always present to the same degree. One thing must always be true, however. Some of all and all of some will be evident as you live out your experience in Christ.

All in all, I think you must make the adjustments to your life that will allow these faith practices to become more and more evident in your life as a believer.

If you have come to the conclusion of this book and you realize that these evidences for the Christian life are absent in your life, I invite you to turn your life over to Christ at this moment. Offer Him your nothing—for you have nothing to offer—and receive His everything—for He has all that you need!

Jesus has paid the full price of redemption for your soul. He died on the cross and rose from the dead that you might be saved. You can receive His salvation today and become gloriously amazed as the evidences for Christianity begin to blossom in the garden of your life.

Please let me know about the decision you have made either to trust Christ as your Savior or to deepen your Christian life through studies like this. You may contact me through one of several social media methods as listed at the end of the next section, About The Author.

You can be a "living martyr" for Christ as you fulfil the mission of being a witness for Him who bought you with such a great price. You can become a proof of Christianity to a doubting world.

ABOUT THE AUTHOR

R.E. CLARK currently serves as an associational missionary in Arkansas. He earned his D.Min. from the Southern Baptist Center in Jacksonville, Florida. He served as a pastor in four churches before beginning his service as the associational missionary to the 69 churches, missions, and ministry points of the Northwest Baptist Association in Bentonville, Arkansas.

His writing comes from life experiences which include over 33 years in ministry. Before his call to ministry he was a business owner. His devotional life deepened and writing career began in 2008 after the death of his wife Kay from Lou Gehrig's Disease. He has written two yearlong devotional books: *Glasses in the Grass: Devotions For My Friends* and *Life Is Not A Snapshot: It's A Mosaic.*

This book is preceded in the series, *Understanding Life's Journey,* by his first Bible study work, *God's Leading: 7 Ways To Know God Is Leading You.* He has also authored a book on revival. *Expecting Revival* includes a history of revival in America, the biblical basis for revival, and a manual for forming teams that will prepare the church for a revival from heaven.

He has been blessed in his second marriage to Trudy. Trudy's first husband, a police officer, was killed in the line of duty. Together they have 8 children, 17 grandchildren, and one great-grandchild. They reside in Centerton, Arkansas.

You may contact the author through the following social media avenues:

Facebook: R.e. Clark
Twitter: GlassesnGrass
Blog: reclarkauthor.com
Email: reclark@reclarkauthor.com